The Ultimate Janitorial Success System

"How My Team Turns Janitorial Customers into Raving Fans and Lifelong Clients"

Glen Springfield

Copyright © 2017 Glen Springfield

All rights reserved.

ISBN-10: 1540421279
ISBN-13: 978-1540421272

DEDICATION

This book is dedicated to my son Samuel.
He is my inspiration. He gives my life meaning.
His childlike innocence, love and emotional
authenticity is rare and precious.

CONTENTS

	Acknowledgments	i
	Preface	Pg 1
1	Introduction	Pg 3
2	Will You Succeed?	Pg 11
3	I Love the Janitorial Business	Pg 21
4	Why Own a Janitorial Business?	Pg 29
5	Recipe For Janitorial Success	Pg 37
6	Unique Product & Production System	Pg 41
7	Labor Strategy	Pg 55
8	Tools & Supply Strategy	Pg 63
9	Supervision & Quality Management	Pg 69
10	Strategic Expansion	Pg 77
11	Customer Acquisition	Pg 107
12	Leadership	Pg 115
13	Your 3 Biggest Difficulties	Pg 119
14	UJSS Conclusion	Pg 133
15	Janitorial Business Coaching	Pg 139
16	How Well Do You Sleep On Stormy Nights?	Pg 143

ACKNOWLEDGMENTS

I would like to acknowledge and thank all of the Janitorial Business Owners and Contractors I've had the privilege of working with over many years. My businesses have been built on the lessons learned from your experiences.

I also want to acknowledge my amazing team at Delta Janitorial Systems, Inc. You guys carry the load so well. I am very proud of you and the brilliant work you do. It is a real delight to come to work because you guys are so much fun. You also give me great peace of mind knowing our business and reputation is in the best of hands.

Thank you all for your dedication and loyalty.

PREFACE

Hello. My name is Glen Springfield and I consider myself to be the luckiest janitor in the world. For the past 40 plus years, I have been hunting down . . . testing . . . and proving little–known ways to literally force janitorial businesses to explode with more customers and higher profits.

I've spent a fortune on experts, consultants and cutting-edge marketing information. I made all the "rookie" mistakes, learned my lessons, fixed my problems and honed the stuff that worked into almost frightening effectiveness.

And it's paid off amazingly well. My "bag of tricks is now bursting with specific "no brainer" ways to get new janitorial accounts at will and drive bottom-line profits through the roof.

It's an actual SYSTEM you can plug into your own janitorial business quickly, easily and without any real financial risk at all.

And it's simple to put this system to work for YOU!

In this book, I'll show you an approach to janitorial business building that will get you as many highly profitable janitorial accounts as you want while making more money in less time.

What you will learn in this book will give you a gigantic advantage allowing you to build a valuable janitorial business very quickly.

To Your Janitorial Success,

Glen Springfield

GLEN SPRINGFIELD

Chapter 1

INTRODUCTION

In the preface of this book I wrote that I considered myself to be the luckiest janitor in the world.

Here Are The Reasons Why:

- I am a high school dropout, former City of Dallas Sanitation Engineer. For those unfamiliar with the term, I was a garbage man.
- I have been broke, buried in massive debt, lived in government housing and held down two jobs that paid practically nothing just to put food on the table.
- I entered the commercial cleaning business washing windows and doing janitorial work for other janitorial companies.
- I started my own commercial cleaning business by buying a few janitorial accounts from one of these companies and cleaning those accounts myself.

- I worked very hard and after 18 years I built that janitorial business into a million dollar a year business.

- After losing that business in a divorce, I built a second multi-million dollar janitorial business in less than a year. It took 18 years to build my first million dollar janitorial business and it took less than a year to build the second one. What changed? Me. With the second business I knew what to do and how to do it to get quick results.

- I have taught others to build million dollar janitorial businesses.

- I have created and documented my business building process into a teachable system called The Ultimate Janitorial Success System.

- The Ultimate Janitorial Success System is simple, doable, repeatable, it works and you can scale your business to any size you want.

Why Should You Listen To Me?

I have been in the janitorial business for more than 40 years. I have built several multimillion dollar janitorial businesses. My companies have contracted thousands of janitorial accounts and worked with thousands of Janitorial Contractors. In that time I've seen many people succeed in the janitorial business. I've seen people make more money than they ever thought possible. I've also seen many people fail.

Some people get into the janitorial business to make a little "extra" money.

A little extra money is always good and almost never bad.

That said, the janitorial industry has a lot more to offer than just a little "extra" money to those ambitious few willing to invest their time and energy into learning the business building principles and taking the steps discussed in this book.

The purpose of this book is to teach you the Ultimate Janitorial Success System. I also want to give you the logic behind the system, so that you'll be able to follow the system with confidence. I want you to understand the system so well that you will not be tempted to deviate and try to take the short cuts that almost always stunt your business growth. In other words I want to "sell" you on the system, so that you have 100% confidence that this is the very best way to operate your business, and in turn you'll be wildly successful.

More Reasons You Should Listen To Me

In working with the successful Janitorial Contractors, and with those that didn't succeed, I have learned a lot. I've seen the attitudes and methods that lead to success and I've seen the attitudes and methods that lead to failure.

When you see the plan that will be laid out for you in this book, you'll be looking at the result of more than 40 years of experience in the janitorial business, plus the experience of thousands of Janitorial Contractors and hundreds of hours dedicated to developing "The Ultimate Janitorial Success System".

But, as well thought out, carefully planned and tested as The Ultimate Janitorial Success System is I realize that we live in a changing world, and the janitorial industry is changing quickly with it. It's becoming a larger and more respected industry. It's becoming more and more profitable.

It's also becoming more and more complex. That means that the development of our system is never complete. And we're working to improve it every day.

Build For The Future

The Ultimate Janitorial Success System that my team and I have developed is in line with where we believe the janitorial industry is going, and it's in line with the regulatory decisions that will be made and enforced in the near future.

Plus, we regularly attend trade shows, conventions and seminars to stay up on the latest in equipment, the latest chemicals and the latest cleaning procedures and technology. We're dedicated to being the best, and providing you with the very best information available, today and in the future.

The lessons that were learned through the blood, sweat and tears of others have been compiled into The Ultimate Janitorial Success System that is presented in this book. It's already been tested. It works. The developmental risks have already been taken for you. There is nothing to figure out on your own. You just use it. And make money.

The information I am sharing in this book is especially important with the current financial threats we are facing today.

What Financial Threats?

The Economy: We can all agree that the economy isn't what it used to be. We hear predictions and affirmations of improvement but are we seeing any benefit from those claims? And even if the economy did improve significantly, for most of us, it wouldn't improve our financial future enough to make a real difference.

Rising Taxes: It seems that taxes and government forced health care are taking more and more of the money that we do manage to make.

Rising Cost of Living: The amount of money that it takes to just survive continues to climb every year. Rent, transportation, food and clothes require more and more money each year.

Decreased Buying Power: How far does your money go nowadays? In my lifetime, the things that make life fun, hobbies, movies, going out to eat – have continued to get more expensive every year. Many people are forced to sit in front of the TV night after night because they can't afford to do anything else.

Job Security: More layoffs and more company closings are in the future. Companies we thought would be around forever are no longer here. Others have been bailed out for the short term by the government but we pay for those bail outs with our tax dollars.

How secure is your current job? How profitable is the company you work for?

Limited Promotion Opportunities: Will climbing the corporate ladder at your work get you to where you want to be financially?

Difficult Workplace: Many people suffer through work daily, miserable in a difficult work place simply because it is too difficult and too risky to try to find a better situation somewhere else.

Unreasonable Bosses: As it becomes more and more difficult for companies to make a profit in our competitive environment, more and more pressure is put on management to lower costs and improve productivity. That means they must demand their personnel produce more work for less money. The choice is to either comply and deal with the abuse or be fired.

Questionable Retirement: At one time, when our economy was strong a person could go to work for a company, put in their time and count on a pension they could retire on. Nowadays that is no longer true. Retirement is questionable at best. Social security benefits are not keeping up with the cost of living so benefits are decreasing annually. Some predict Social Security will collapse under the load of its obligations that are no longer funded.

So, how do we deal with these overwhelming financial threats?

Here's How!

- First, you must get "real" with yourself. Stop depending entirely on your job to achieve your financial goals.

- Second, you must begin to direct at least a portion of your efforts into building your own business, which will . . .

- Third, increase your income and build an asset that can be sold at some point in the future.

Everyone knows that owning a janitorial business can be very profitable.

In every major city there are many successful janitorial businesses. Millions upon millions of dollars are spent on office cleaning services every single year. That means that a lot of people just like you and I are making a lot of money by providing janitorial services to their communities.

In almost every group that I speak to there will be several people that are acquainted with at least one very successful janitorial business owner.

Are these successful janitorial business owners particularly smart? Are they highly educated? Are they better looking than most? In most cases the answer to those questions is NO! They are, for the most part very ordinary. So, how did they do it? How did they build their own successful janitorial business?

A better question to focus on is this:

"Can You Build A Successful Janitorial Business Of Your Own?"

You will definitely need the right information, the right recipe, the right ingredients and a lot of hard work.

That said, *"Will YOU be successful and should you even try?"*

I have written Chapter 2 to help you answer that important question.

Things To Remember:

- Today we are confronted with a host of very real financial threats that will only get worse as time progresses.

- The world has changed. A job alone no longer offers long term security or advancement.

- You don't have to be stuck where you are. You can take action and change your outcome.

- Building a janitorial business offers a true "rags to riches" opportunity for those with the right characteristics and attributes.

- There is a specific path to follow in building a successful janitorial business that removes most of the risk and accelerates growth.

Chapter 2

WILL YOU SUCCEED?

"Will You Succeed In Building a Successful Janitorial Business?"

Succeeding in Your Own Janitorial Business Requires a Certain Perspective, Mindset and Attitude. Do You Have What It Takes?

The purpose of this chapter is to give you the information you need in order to make a quick, accurate decision about whether or not you **should** attempt to build your own janitorial business or whether you should look elsewhere for your dream business.

If...

If you can build a solid, successful janitorial business, make a lot of money, build security for yourself and your family and put all of that on autopilot then you ought to give it all you've got and make it happen.

But...

If building a janitorial business would cause you to lose time, lose money, lose sleep, lose peace of mind and then fail to achieve your business building goals - then it's something that you should not do.

So how do you know if you will succeed or fail in your own janitorial business?

First, Understand Why Janitorial Businesses Exist:

Janitorial Businesses provide cleaning services to facilities and businesses that do not want to provide those cleaning services for themselves.

- **They don't want to empty their own trash.**
- They don't want to dust their own furniture.
- **They don't want to clean up cup rings and small spills.**
- They don't want to vacuum their own carpet.
- **They don't want to sweep and mop their own floors.**
- And they especially don't want to clean their own restrooms.

Those businesses would prefer to come to work in the morning and find:

- Empty trash cans with clean liners.
- **Dust free furniture, equipment, wall hangings, etc.**
- Clean work surfaces.
- **Freshly vacuumed carpets.**
- Clean, shiny floors.

- **Clean and disinfected restrooms.**

Of course, this would be their experience only after a competent janitorial service had serviced the facility the previous evening.

In order to enjoy these luxuries and not burden their own staff with these chores, businesses are willing to pay janitorial services quite handsomely to take care of office and restroom cleaning.

It is a perk to employees to enjoy clean offices and restrooms without having to do those chores themselves. It also allows the employees of a business to work on those items that serve their employer best in driving revenue and serving their own customers.

Reasons Why Janitorial Services Fail:

We've addressed why a business or facility uses a janitorial service and what a business or facility expects from their janitorial service. Now let's take an honest look at how janitorial services lose their customers.

Things That Get Janitorial Services Fired:

- Helping themselves to candy, coffee and sodas that are intended for their employees and customers.

- **Unauthorized use of their office equipment like telephones, computers, printers, copy machines and fax machines.**

- Using the personal property of their customers personnel like playing their radios etc.

- **Security problems like leaving doors unlocked that are supposed to be secured.**

- Losing their keys and access cards.

- **Adjusting their thermostats.**

- Smoking in or outside of their facility.

- **Unprofessional grooming and dress. Looking sloppy or scary.**

- Stealing.

- **Failing to provide the agreed upon service on the agreed upon schedule.**

New janitorial businesses fail because they fail to deliver those things that janitorial customers wanted and expected when they hired the janitorial service.

Janitorial Customers Will Not Tolerate Excuses.

They Don't Care If:

- Your car broke down

- **Your kid got sick**

- You got sick

- **Somebody in your family died**

- You didn't have gas money

- **You had a flat tire**

- You got your days mixed up

- **You don't like driving in the rain**

- There might be a freeze tonight

- **Your tires aren't in good condition**

They simply want the janitorial services they contracted for, delivered as agreed.

Benjamin Franklin said "He that is good for making excuses is seldom good for anything else".

The Simple But Profound Truth About Janitorial Success!

To the best of my understanding and ability, painfully learned from my 40 plus years in the business, I have listed the reasons that facilities and businesses use janitorial services. I have listed, in general, what janitorial customers expect from their janitorial vendors. If those expectations seem unreasonable to you, then **owning a janitorial business is a bad idea for you.**

If that list of reasons why janitorial services get fired seems a little **harsh** to you then **owning a janitorial business is a bad idea for you.**

I also listed a myriad of excuses that have been used to explain janitorial non-performance and bad performance. If those excuses seem reasonable to you then **owning a janitorial business is a bad idea for you.**

On the other hand, if the janitorial client expectations I listed seem reasonable to you and if you believe that you can meet or exceed these client expectations then there is a very good reason to believe that **you will likely do well in your own janitorial business.**

If the list of reasons why janitorial services get fired seem reasonable to you then you are on the same page as most janitorial clients which is another reason **you will likely do well in your own janitorial business.**

If that list of janitorial non-performance excuses seems lame to you then that is even one more reason to believe that **you will do well in your own janitorial business.** Janitorial Success is not complicated. Keep your customers happy and you will get more customers. Disappoint your customers and you will lose your customers and your business.

This simple but profound truth applies to all businesses not just a janitorial business. A janitorial business of your own offers greater opportunity because there are so many people in this business that simply don't get it. It's hard to fail in the janitorial business by delivering great janitorial services.

At this point you should have a pretty good idea if you have the right values and mindset for janitorial business success. If you believe you have the right mindset, you should also carefully consider the following.

If you answer "NO" to any of the following questions then a janitorial business is probably not right for you at this time.

- **Are You Healthy?** Do you have health problems that would prevent you from following and teaching a strict cleaning system?
- **Are You Financially Stable?** When you start a business there is a delay between the work you do and the money you receive for the work. Janitorial accounts typically pay monthly and not always on time. You will need either savings or income from another source to get started.
- **Are You Easy To Work With?** Difficult people do not do well in this business. If you are prone to emotional outburst, get mad or angry easily, this is not the right business for you.
- **Do You Have a Strong Work Ethic?** People that put what they are "getting" ahead of what they are "giving" will not do well in business for themselves.

- **Are You Honest and Dependable?** Integrity is essential in business. If your integrity becomes compromised then working relationships fall apart. Accounts will be lost and you will suffer financial loss.

- **Do You Have A Burning Desire To Build Your Own Janitorial Business?** Desire is the element that fuels your success and your business. Without real desire people can't finish what they have started. Quitters never win. Winners never quit.

- **Do You Enjoy and Are You Willing To Help Others?** The Mastermind Principle is a very large element in successful business building. If you are not willing to engage with, work with and help others succeed then you will have a more difficult and longer journey to business building success. If you are a loner and like working alone; if you think that you don't need help from others and that you can do it all on your own then you will be fighting an uphill battle.

Success Starts In Your Imagination.

If you can't visualize success then you certainly can't achieve success. Take a moment or two to put your imagination to work. It is very important that you learn to do this regularly. Success begins in your imagination and works its way out.

Imagine How Your Life Would Be Different If:

- You didn't have to go to work tomorrow?
- You didn't have to worry about paying the bills?
- You had more time with your family?
- You had money for nice cars, a nice house, nice vacations?

- You owned a business that became more valuable each year and could be sold for a windfall profit?
- You owned a business that worked for you, instead of you working for someone else's business?

Imagine Your Janitorial Business

- Brings in lots of money every month
- Is growing in value and can be sold for a big payday
- Is stable in almost any economy
- Provides a valuable service to the community
- Wins you the respect and admiration of your peers
- Provides work to many who need jobs
- Pays for vacations, cruises, cars, homes, college educations and all of the finer things in life
- Gives you more time for your family
- Provides security for yourself and your family
- Gives you and your family options that are only available to those that are financially independent

Perform this imagination exercise daily with faith and you will be amazed how fast you will progress toward your goals.

Things To Remember:

- It's important to understand why facilities and businesses use janitorial services and what they expect.
- There a list of specific behaviors that get janitorial services fired.
- Janitorial clients will not accept excuses for poor service.

- Success starts in your imagination. Imagination exercises are in important element to success.

- There are specific personal attributes that are required for your janitorial business building efforts to succeed.

- A successful janitorial business will change your life.

Chapter 3

I LOVE THE JANITORIAL BUSINESS

I love the janitorial business because it offers so much opportunity for people who find themselves in disadvantaged situations. Martin Luther King, in his "I have a dream" speech, said that he looked forward to a day when people would be judged by the "content of their character rather than the color of their skin".

Sadly, most people in disadvantaged situations are missing the important success element of character. However, for those that exercise good character in their lives, a janitorial business offers many advantages over just about every other kind of business on the planet.

Here are 9 Good Reasons to Start a Janitorial Business:

The 1st reason to start your own janitorial business is to create a second income. Now why would anyone want a second income?

The reason is there are a lot of financial threats in our current economy that make it unsafe to depend on a single income from a job. I discussed those in a previous chapter. As a reminder here's a short list.

- The Economy. We can all agree that the economy isn't what it used to be.
- Rising Taxes that erode our buying power.
- Inflation. "Things" cost more every year.
- Job Security. How secure is your current job?
- Lack of Job Advancement Opportunities.
- Hostile Unpleasant Work Place.
- Difficult Bosses and Unreasonable Demands.
- Questionable Retirement.

The 2nd good reason to start a janitorial business is that it's a very simple business.

Get janitorial accounts, Get those janitorial accounts cleaned. Get paid. Simple.

The 3rd good reason to start a janitorial business is that it can be started part time. The business can start small and expand until it gets big enough to replace a job. It can keep growing year by year and become huge.

The 4th good reason to start a janitorial business is low overhead. Compared to other kinds of businesses, a janitorial business has very low overhead. You don't have to rent a big store front or buy a ton of inventory. You can keep expenses low and profits high.

The 5th good reason to start a janitorial business is low risk. About the only way to fail in the janitorial business is to deliver bad service. If you deliver bad services then you will fail. But if you deliver great services you will succeed. In the janitorial business, success is totally up to you.

The 6th good reason to start a janitorial business is the short learning curve. Don't get me wrong. There is a lot to learn but in the janitorial business you can learn as you earn. The only thing you need to learn to get started is how to clean and most of us have been cleaning our whole lives.

The 7th good reason to start a janitorial business is the extremely low investment and startup cost.

Many businesses require big bucks to get started like restaurants and retail stores. In the janitorial business all it takes is a thousand dollars of commercial cleaning equipment and something to clean.

The 8th good reason to start a janitorial business is that it generates cash fast. Many businesses have to be in business a year or more to start making money.

In the janitorial business you can have money rolling within just a few months.

The 9th and best reason to build a janitorial business of your own is that they are worth a lot of money! Most people fail to understand that janitorial businesses are regularly bought and sold.

The larger a janitorial business becomes, the more profit it will typically generate. The more profit it generates, the more valuable it becomes when it's time to sell.

I urge everyone to Google the term "Janitorial Business For Sale". Take a look at the janitorial services that are for sale and take note of how they are being valued.

I will give you a few examples of what I found last time I did this exercise.

Example #1:

Janitorial Business For Sale Listing 318628

- Sales: $512,239
- Profits: $ 124,000
- Profit Type: Sellers discretionary cash flow. (SDCF)
- Asking Price: $325,000

This business is averaging $42,686 each month. With an asking price of $325,000 they are asking 7.16 times the average monthly billing or 2.16 times the annual profit.

Example #2:

Janitorial Business For Sale Listing 339900

- Sales: $145,568
- Profits: $50,101
- Profit Type: Cash Flow
- Asking Price: $110,000

This business is averaging $12,132 each month. With an asking price of $145,568 they are asking 9.06 times the average monthly billing or 2.19 times the annual profit.

Example #3:

Janitorial Business For Sale Listing 333286

- Sales: $52,148

- Profits: $46,748
- Profit Type: Sellers discretionary cash flow. (SDCF)
- Asking Price: $110,000

This business is averaging $4,345 each month. With an asking price of $52,148 they are asking 13.08 times the average monthly billing or 1.28 times the annual profit. In this case the owner is doing all of the work so the profit margin appears to be higher than normal.

Example #4:

Janitorial Business For Sale Listing 331823

- Sales: $612,942
- Profits: $195,000
- Profit Type: Cash Flow
- Asking Price: $450,000

This business is averaging $51,078 each month. With an asking price of $450,000 they are asking 8.81 times the average monthly billing or 2.3 times the annual profit.

Example #5:

Janitorial Business For Sale Listing 266849

- Sales: $308,000
- Profits: $101,000
- Profit Type: Cash Flow
- Asking Price: $200,000

This business is averaging $25,666 each month. With an asking price of $200,000 they are asking 7.79 times the average monthly billing or 1.98 times the annual profit. This business is a resale of a janitorial franchise located in Florida.

As you can see from these examples, Janitorial Businesses are regularly valued at 7 to 9 times their monthly gross income or 2 times their annual profits.

What Does That Mean For You?

- Most people in the janitorial business are only looking at how much they make each month and ignore how much their business can be sold for.

- When you understand that the big money is in the equity, you look at and you treat your business differently. This is more than a job.

- You can make good money from operating and building a janitorial business and . . .

- Have a giant payday when you sell it.

Is it possible that you could build a valuable and successful janitorial business:

- Without a Large Investment?

- Without Risk?

- Without Selling?

- Without Marketing Skills?

- Without Business Experience?

With the simple recipe you will learn in this book plus some honest effort and hard work on your part, I believe you can. I haven't met anyone who followed this recipe who has failed so far.

Things To Remember:

- There are nine great reasons to start and grow a janitorial business of your own.

- A janitorial business is one of the easiest and least expensive businesses to start.

- The biggest benefit to building your own janitorial business is the equity that you build in your business.

- Janitorial businesses sell for lots of money.

- You can make great money while you're building a business and if you build your business right, you can have a giant payday when you sell.

- There is a simple recipe that anyone can follow to build their own successful janitorial business.

Chapter 4

WHY OWN A JANITORIAL BUSINESS?

Before we jump into the meat of The Ultimate Janitorial Success System I want to put owning your own profitable janitorial business in proper perspective by taking a look at some other professions.

Profession	Education	Average Income	Starting Income
Doctor	10 Years	$156,000	$40,000 to $50,000
Surgeon	12 to 15 Years	$346,000	$280,000
Psychologist	9 to 11 Years	$87,000	$40,000

Lawyer	7 Years	$75,000	$35,000
CPA	4 Years	$74,000	$41,000

The chart above will help you compare the professional incomes and educational requirements of some much respected professions to the opportunity of owning your own profitable janitorial business. For someone to become a Medical Doctor they are in training for at least 10 years. That's 10 years without making any money. They also have to pay their living expenses for that time and pay for college and medical school.

That is a huge investment of time, energy and money. Then their starting income is only about $40,000 to $50,000 until they finish their residency. Even after they are well established their average income is only $156,000.

If someone starts their own janitorial business they begin making money their very first year. Their startup expenses are a tiny fraction of the cost to become a Doctor. And if they follow The Ultimate Janitorial Success System, within 10 years they will be making far more money than a typical Doctor.

A surgeon has an even greater investment than a Medical Doctor. They are in training for 12 to 15 years. The average income of a surgeon is $346,000 but they went 12 long years without making any money from being a surgeon. And their debt from medical school is even higher than a Medical Doctor's.

To become a Psychologist the investment is 9 to 11 years plus living expenses plus college and medical school. The average Psychologist starts in the $40,000 range and builds up to an average of $87,000 a year. It will take them many years to pay off their student loans.

If I told you that to start a janitorial business you would have to go into massive debt and make no money for almost 10 years you probably wouldn't be interested. I don't blame you. But that is the kind of investment people make in order to start a medical practice.

How long does it take to become a lawyer? It takes 7 years to become a lawyer; Four years of college plus three years of law school. How much does an average lawyer make? The average attorney makes about $75,000 a year.

That is still too large of an investment and too long before making any money for me. A profitable janitorial business has far more potential.

How long does it take to become a CPA? You can become a CPA with a regular four year degree if you have twenty-six hours of accounting. How much does an average CPA make? The average CPA makes about $74,000 a year but they start out making around $41,000 a year.

Well. These are some pretty respected professions and some pretty respectable incomes. The point of this exercise is this. Most professional incomes require a lot of training. Some of them require years and years of training. And even after years and years of training, for most professions, they don't make a lot of money immediately. It takes a while to build up a practice.

You also have to factor in that they made zero while they were spending years in school. Not only that, most of them owe massive student loans that have to be repaid.

Owning your own profitable janitorial business requires a much smaller investment, generates income almost immediately and has the potential to grow as large as you want it to.

Just like any of these other professions, you have to put something into your business before you get anything out of it. And the more you put into it, the more you put into your personal and professional development, the more success you'll have in your business.

Owning your own profitable janitorial business has one major advantage over all of these professions. If you think about it, all of these professionals are trading hours for dollars. If they quit providing their services, they quit getting paid.

Surgeons have to perform surgery, doctors have to see patients, lawyers have to try cases and CPA's have to crunch numbers. There is no residual income from any of these professions.

In this book, I'm going to show you how to build a janitorial business that can provide you a professional income even after you quit working in the business. Now, nobody said it was going to be easy. I can guarantee you, that at times, it'll be tough. It will be so tough that some of you may quit. But I can also guarantee that for those of you who stick with it and succeed, it'll be worth it.

A Worthy Goal

You should set out on this venture knowing that you are pursuing a worthy goal. You and your business will grow year after year. You'll employ many people over the years. You'll touch many lives. You'll build knowledge and skills in many areas. In order to succeed, you'll become a good business person.

It doesn't really matter how much you know or how much experience you have to begin with. Only that you start and you always move forward. The only way to fail is to quit. All set backs are only temporary. They're lessons to be learned on the road to success.

Your business will be one of your greatest teachers and it will become one of your greatest prides. Sometimes it will require a lot of patience. Sometimes things won't develop as fast as you want them to. It's then that I want you to think of some of these professions, and the years of training that were invested.

Every year in business is an investment in the next year. Every day, every week, every month is an investment in your future. It's a never ending school. What you will become as a result of succeeding in this business, is of far greater value than the money you'll make.

As you can see, I think a lot of this business. I think it's a precious opportunity for many people to get out of a rut and do something exciting and adventurous; to do something fun; to build something worthwhile; to invest their time and resources into something that can pay them back for a lifetime.

Welcome to the Janitorial Business. Welcome to The Ultimate Janitorial Success System.

What Is The Difference Between a Service and a Business?

A service is something that you do. Whether you are a doctor, a dentist, an attorney, a hair cutter or a janitor, a service is something that you do. A business does not require you to provide the service or produce a product.

What Is A Business?

Here is a simple definition:

A business is a profit seeking enterprise that's involved in the production of a service or a product through a combination of equipment, materials and labor.

Does that make sense?

So, to have a business all you do is combine equipment, materials and labor to produce a product or a service and you have a business. That sounds pretty easy.

Good Business VS Bad Business

Now there are good businesses and bad businesses. What would some characteristics of a good business be?

Typical Characteristics of a Good Business.

- A good business must be profitable. Unprofitable businesses go bankrupt. The main reason that a business is started is to produce a profit for the owners.

- Good businesses are stable. If a business is stable, profits are reliable and the business is fulfilling its purpose.

- Good businesses produce quality products and services. Poor quality ruins reputations, relationships and leads to business failure.

- Good businesses have good employees. Good employees take care of customers and care about the quality of their work and contribution.

- Good businesses have good employee morale. Employees have positive and pleasant attitudes.

- A good business serves the community by providing great products or services along with providing opportunities and jobs.

It stands to reason then, that a bad business would have the opposite of one or more of these characteristics.

A bad business would be unprofitable, or unstable, or produce poor quality, or have bad employees or have bad employee moral or I guess a real bad business would have all of these. That doesn't sound like a business that I would want to be a part of. How about you?

Definition Of A Great Business.

Here is the definition of a business that I'd like to own.

A fool proof system that produces a consistent, high quality service or product through a combination of materials, labor and equipment at a price the market is willing to pay, while generating a reasonable profit for the owners.

Does that sound like a great business that you would like to own?

Things To Remember:

- A janitorial business will make more money faster than many well respected professional careers requiring years of education.

- There is a big difference between a service and a business.

- There is a big difference between a business and a great business.

Chapter 5

RECIPE FOR JANITORIAL SUCCESS

In this chapter, I'm going to begin to unpack my approach to janitorial business building that allows my teams to get all the janitorial accounts they want while generating more money in less time.

This approach will give anyone a gigantic advantage and allow them to build a valuable janitorial business far faster and with far less effort.

Wouldn't you like to know a proven recipe that will produce a great janitorial business as described above?

Well then read on.

The Ultimate Janitorial Success System has seven major ingredients. I'll give you the ingredients first. Then I'll address each ingredient individually. Each of these ingredients is extremely important. I call them major ingredients because if any single one of them is missing, you'll have business failure.

You might call them the essential ingredients. Of course there are hundreds of minor ingredients that make things easier or more successful. We can't cover all of those possibilities in a single book. But the essential ingredients are all here.

The UJSS Ingredient List:

Ingredient #1: A Unique Product and Production System.

You're in the janitorial business. As a business owner you will need a clearly defined method of production that will produce the services you're in business to provide. It must produce consistent quality and be scalable.

Ingredient #2: A Labor Strategy

You need willing workers. For most people who get in this business, to begin with, they are the willing workers. And that's good, but to grow, you must be able to go beyond that. We'll talk about the different ways to compensate workers and what workers need in order to be successful. You will need an effective strategy for labor.

Ingredient #3: An Equipment And Supply Strategy

We'll talk about what supplies and equipment you'll need plus we'll talk about a strategy for inventory, storage, maintenance and laundry.

Ingredient #4: A Supervision And Quality Control Strategy

We'll talk about the need for supervision, what effective supervision is, and what ineffective supervision is. I think you'll be surprised by the information I'll give you. You'll have a clear and effective strategy for supervision.

Ingredient #5: A Solid Business Foundation and Growth Plan

In order to build a successful business you need a plan. Like a battle plan, you need to know what you are trying to do and how you intend to do it. You need to know what it will look like when you're finished and what it will look like at the different stages of growth.

Your company's written values and beliefs are like the rules of war. They are declarations of what you want your company to stand for and how you want your company to operate. Your company's written Value and Belief Statements will dictate the standards and the management strategy you will use to run your business.

I'll lay out the basics of written Value and Belief Statements that you can use as a starter and then you can personalize them to make them your own for your business.

Then I'll lay out a business growth plan step by step. This is the battle plan that you can use to build your janitorial empire. I'll incorporate the first five ingredients into a solid game plan.

Ingredient #6 Is Customers.

To be successful you have to have customers. To grow you need a steady supply of new customers. This calls for a new customer strategy. I will present you with three strategies for getting all of the janitorial clients you will ever want.

Ingredient #7 Is Leadership.

We'll talk about the need to have a vision and how important it is to communicate that vision throughout the organization. We'll give you a leadership strategy.

Then with your unique product and production system, your labor strategy, your equipment and supply strategy, your supervision strategy, your new business building strategy, your written value and belief statements, your new customer strategy and your leadership strategy you'll have the essentials you need to start building your business.

In the following chapters I'll unwrap each of these important ingredients.

Things To Remember:

- The Ultimate Janitorial Success System is a recipe with seven essential ingredients.

Chapter 6

UNIQUE PRODUCT & PRODUCTION SYSTEM

Consider This Question For A Moment.

What do you think is the difference between a business that is "just getting by" and a business that is really thriving?

Often It Is Their Core Offer - Their USP

What's a USP? USP is an acronym for Unique Selling Proposition.

For many companies their USP has been the difference that turned imminent failure into fantastic success.

Example # 1:

Domino's Pizza wasn't originally very successful. One of the partners (a brother) actually quit because the business was so unsuccessful. It was a small pizza shop near a college that was barely getting by. The owner was sleeping in the shop at night because he couldn't afford an apartment.

Then, an almost magical thing happened. The owner discovered the magic of the right USP (Unique Selling Proposition).

"Fresh, Hot Pizza, Delivered In 30 Minutes Or Less...Guaranteed."

That USP put Domino's Pizza on the map. It distinguished them from everyone else and offered a compelling reason to choose Domino's over every other pizza delivery option available. And at the time, if the delivery was late, the pizza was free. That really appealed to college students.

Example #2:

Federal Express was on the verge of bankruptcy when it discovered its magical USP (Unique Selling Proposition).

"When It Absolutely, Positively Has To Get There Overnight."

This company was competing with the US Post Office and losing money like crazy. They were out of cash and desperate. They began to advertise this USP and turned the company around and into a profitable, thriving business.

More Examples:

M&M's – Melts In Your Mouth, Not In Your Hand.

Subway – Eat Fresh

Burger King – "Have It Your Way"

You can look at any fast food franchise and quickly identify how they differentiate themselves from all of the other fast food franchises.

Upon Careful Examination You Will Find That The Businesses That Thrive:

- Focus on a single unique benefit that differentiates them from the other options available to the consumer.
- Their USP is one that resonates with their market.
- Communicate their differentiating benefit very concisely.
- They focus on strengthening their unique benefit.
- They don't try to compete on everyone else's USP.

Considering the above to be true, I focused on developing and testing USP's for the janitorial business until I found one that resonates with my market.

"Better Tools, Better Cleaning".

Yes, I borrowed from Papa John's Pizza "Better Ingredients, Better Pizza".

But I tested many before I settled on Better Tools, Better Cleaning.

I discovered that the only thing that really matters to clients is how economically and how thoroughly we clean.

I Reasoned:

- The Only Way To Provide Economy Would Be To Clean Significantly Faster Than Conventional Competitors.
- Faster Cleaning Must Also Be More Thorough.
- Quality Must Be Enhanced, Not Sacrificed.
- These Goals Can Only Be Achieved Through Better Science, Better Technology, Better Tools and More Efficient Cleaning Processes.

With that clear and focused understanding, I started a very serious Research and Development Process to develop the fastest and most thorough cleaning system possible. This project involved testing hundreds of tools, products and processes.

The Results Exceeded Even My Own Expectations:

- 12% Faster Tool Belt System
- 35% Faster Dusting
- 50% Faster Surface And Glass Cleaning
- 65% Faster Mopping
- 100% Faster Vacuum/Spot Cleaning System

If Your Janitorial Service Could Clean 1/3 Faster Than Other Janitorial Services, What Would That Mean To You?

- Would you make more money in less time?
- Could you offer more competitive pricing?
- Would that result in more business?
- Could you pay your staff better since they're more productive?
- Would better pay attract better staff?
- Would better staff be more consistent, more reliable and dependable, easier to manage causing less stress?
- Would cleaning faster allow more time for detail cleaning?
- Would more detail cleaning increase account satisfaction and retention?

The answer to all of these questions is "yes", but that "yes" is contingent on the presumed fact that we can really clean 1/3 faster than our competition without compromising quality.

So let's take a quick look at where we were able to save time and improve efficiency.

12% Faster Tool Belt System:

Most janitorial services carry their tools on their maid cart or trash barrel. You've probably used or seen the trash barrel caddies or the aprons that hang on trash barrels. This is an inefficient system that causes workers to take many extra steps every night retrieving tools and products.

Think of all of the professional trades that use tool belts. Carpenters do. Phone installers do. Electricians do. Cable guys do plus many, many more.

Why Do They All Use Tool Belts?

The answer is simple. Having their tools where they can easily reach them, without looking, speeds up their work process and makes their work easier to perform.

All of these professionals could just as well carry their tools in a tray or a bucket or on a cart, but that would be slow and clumsy. Tool belts help them get more work done in less time with less effort. It makes their work life easier. Our janitorial tool belts do the same thing.

Here's What A Few Believers Have To Say:

William Emerson ...

Using a tool belt is pretty cool. Electricians and cable guys use tool belts. I'm a professional too. When I need a tool, I have it right there on me. This saves a lot steps and time. I have more time to clean more accounts and make more money.

Mike Ciulla ...

I don't know why it took so long for someone to figure out it's a huge advantage for a janitor to have a tool belt to carry his tools. Its human nature to forget and before I started using a tool belt, sometimes when I needed a certain tool and that tool would be on my cart, I would come back to it when I was done doing what I was doing. Unfortunately, sometimes I would forget. Now, I don't forget because my tools are on my tool belt.

35% Faster Dusting

Everyone is familiar with the lamb's wool duster. It's been the tool of choice for many years but it has a lot of short comings. The duster we use blows it away.

When someone sees a side by side demonstration of our Dusting System, they immediately see how much faster and more thorough the our system is over conventional tools. It's no contest.

Anthony Crenshaw ....

The Clean-Fast duster has way more advantages over all the other ways to dust, especially the lamb's wool duster. My clients love my dusting. It's a lot faster and better.

They say the way we dust is one of the main reasons they went with us over our competition.

Floyd Patterson....

I have been cleaning for over 15 years and prior to becoming a Clean-Fast provider I had always dusted just like everyone else, using a lamb's wool duster or a cloth.

It was basically just a losing battle before the Clean-Fast duster. It is so effective, that I actually use it to clean my own home. After using a Clean-Fast Duster, it's hard to think about using anything else.

50% Faster Surface Cleaning.

The way most people clean surfaces is by spray cleaning. They spray and they wipe. The solution may be different or the cloth may be different but it is still spray cleaning with all of its challenges.

- Filling and spilling
- Bottles stop working
- Bottles have to be primed.
- Bottles break sometimes causing spills
- Overspray
- Etc.

Our surface cleaning system has eliminated spray cleaning and replaced it with a process that is easier, less expensive, faster and has none of the problems listed above.

Orlando Rodriguez....

Using the Clean-Fast Surface Cleaning System is so much faster and better than using a spray bottle and paper towels to wipe surfaces. It was so frustrating when my spray bottle would malfunction which happened often. I love the Clean-Fast Surface Cleaning System.

Eddie Moore ...

The Clean-Fast surface cleaning system blows away every other surface cleaning system.

You have the pre-treated cloths, the dry polish cloths, and my favorite is the speed trowel. I love using it for big conference tables. Nothing else even comes close to it.

65% Faster Mopping

Most janitorial services are still using string mops, mop buckets and wringers. This method of mopping is slow, works poorly and causes a lot of cross contamination between areas.

Our mopping system doesn't use string mops, mop buckets or wringers. It eliminates cross contamination and does a better job in less time.

Courtney Bell ...

The traditional way of mopping with a mop bucket and wringer cannot compete with the Clean-Fast mopping system. There is no on site prep. This system saves me so much time and money. All my clients love their clean floors.

Preston Johnson ...

I just got in this business a few months ago but I've used a mop bucket and wringer throughout my life and comparing that with the Clean-Fast mopping system is laughable and not really fair.

100% Faster Vacuum/Spot Cleaning

Back pack vacuums have been around for more than 20 years but a large part of the janitorial industry is still using uprights. Uprights are slow and do an inferior job. The wrong backpack vacuum with the wrong tools isn't much better than an upright vacuum.

But, the right backpack vacuum with the right tools can be more than twice as fast as an upright or a backpack with poor tools or poor technique.

Carpet spot cleaning used to be such a pain that most services simply don't do it. As a result, janitorial clients look at those carpet spills and spots every day and become more and more dissatisfied with their janitorial service.

Our Carpet Spot Cleaning System takes only seconds per spot and is performed at the same time the vacuuming is being performed so there are no extra trips to go back and deal with a carpet spot or spill.

Anthony Crenshaw ...

Being an ex-franchise owner with another janitorial company had a lot of challenges. It was difficult keeping my clients consistently happy. And I gave it everything I had. I just did not have the right tools. I used traditional tools, like everyone else. I lost accounts and that business eventually failed. I have been a Clean-Fast Provider for 5 months now. My buildings are extremely clean, I'm succeeding and my clients love me. It's not me though it's just the Clean-Fast tools and system.

Marcus Brandon ...

I am a business owner but new to this industry, so I was really impressed and excited with the Clean-Fast System.

Not only was I going to be able to provide superior cleaning than my competition, but in doing so, I was actually going to be able to lower my labor cost.

What else could I ask for other than this. It's a definite Win-Win!

The Clean-Fast Tools and System Produce a Consistent:

- 12% Increase In Speed and Productivity Through The Tool Belt System
- 35% Faster Dusting
- 50% Faster Surface Cleaning
- 65% Faster Mopping
- 100% Faster Vacuum/Spot Cleaning

Here's The Question

If your janitorial cleaning system was one third faster and more thorough than conventional janitorial services, could you provide great janitorial services?

Well, your unique service and highly defined production system is the first ingredient in The Ultimate Janitorial Success System Recipe.

Why is a highly defined production system so important?

Let me explain. Have you ever known someone who was a really good baker?

If you watch a really good cook you would see that they don't always go by an exact recipe. If they're baking cookies they might start with the flour, add the eggs, sugar, salt, baking powder and the other ingredients but they won't necessarily measure things precisely.

They just put so much of this and about this much of that and they mix it up, bake it, and out comes perfect cookies. They can do it time after time and get perfect cookies every time. Now picture this. This person is a good baker. This person knows how to make cookies. They have their own method and it works.

Now, what if this person had to bake 100,000 cookies in a day, using 100 employees? How would their under defined method work then? Would they tell their employees just use a little of this and a little of that until it looks right then bake them?

Of course not, but if they did, what do you think the results would be? To bake 100,000 cookies in a day, using a hundred employees, you would need a highly defined system. You would need organization and very specific procedures. Everything would have to be meticulously measured to ensure that the end product was what it was intended to be. Does that make sense?

So if you're doing everything yourself, you may get away with following a fairly loose system and perhaps you will get good results if you are a master of your craft. But if you're getting things done through other people, you need a very tight system. You need very specific job descriptions, very specific methods and very specific techniques.

Now let's go back to the master baker who bakes cookies a few dozen at a time and does everything himself. How does that person build up to 100 employees baking 100,000 cookies a day?

Build On A Solid Foundation

The master baker starts, of course, with one employee. Now if that new employee observes the master baker, baking without measuring, what will the new employee believe about following a precise system? It's the old "do as I say, not as I do" routine.

Experts say that 94% of communication is non-verbal. Through observation the new employee has formed some very dangerous beliefs. The new employee may do as he is told, but he now has a belief about the necessity of accurate and careful measurements. He believes that they aren't really necessary, if you're good enough

That belief will surface at one time or another in the production process. That belief will also be transferred to new personnel. That collective belief will cause so much variation in the production system that the whole process will be out of control.

That one inaccurate belief could put the entire company out of business. And where did it start? It started with the master baker.

Variation Is The Enemy

Variation is a major cause of poor quality. I'm talking about variation in production methods and techniques. Poor quality is a major cause of business failure. So, in your company, the less variation there is in following the production system, the more successful your company will be.

The production system that we've developed is called the Clean-Fast Office Cleaning System. It's the product of over 30 years of research and development. It's so important to my businesses that it has its own video training program.

I'm not saying that this system is the only way to clean a building. We know that just like master bakers who do many things different and all get good results, there are master cleaners, if you will, that can do many things differently and all get good results.

But, when it comes to a system that can be taught and used by hundreds of employees, this system is state of the art. When this system is used exactly, with no deviation, variation in results will be very small and overall quality will be very high.

I want to urge you to make a commitment to follow a strict cleaning system exactly as it is defined, without deviation. Make it a part of you. Learn it down to the smallest detail.

"Know this; if you vary from your production system just a little, your staff will vary from your production system a lot."

Predictable Success

In my business, almost every time we have a complaint or a problem with the quality of work, invariably it is because the production system was not followed. We can even predict the quality of work a particular team leader will produce over the long run, simply by their attitude toward following the production system without deviation.

If they have a casual attitude toward following production system deviation, we know that when they start adding team members, they will experience quality problems. We know that if they are strict in following the production system, and insist that everyone on their team follow the system exactly, they will produce very high quality in the field.

A strict well defined Cleaning System is essential to your janitorial business success. As business owners, our job is to make sure that our production system stays "state of the art". We are always on the lookout for new techniques, new equipment, new chemicals and new theories of management all the time. You should be too!

Things To Remember:

- Successful businesses have a Unique Selling Proposition that makes them stand out from their competition.

- You can make your services unique with better tools and technology.

- Modeling desired behavior is essential.

- Variation is the enemy.

- Success and failure are both predictable.

GLEN SPRINGFIELD

Chapter 7

LABOR STRATEGY

Next on our list of ingredients is labor. By labor we're talking about willing workers. You can't have a company unless you have willing workers. A willing worker is defined as someone who wants their job, is committed to doing their best each and every day, and is committed to continuous improvement.

Where Do You Find Willing Workers?

How do you attract and hire willing workers? Well, like in most things you have to offer something of value in order to get something of value. So let's look at this from a workers point of view.

What do good workers want in a job?

1. Would you agree that most people want to be paid?
2. How about stability? Everyone wants stability. They want to know that their job will be there tomorrow and that the checks they receive will be good.

3. Most people are interested in a future, the opportunity to advance and make more money in the future.

4. Most people want good tools to work with. Nothing is more frustrating than trying to do good work, but you can't because you don't have the right tools or the right equipment.

5. How about clear instructions. If you don't have clear instructions, a person can work very hard for a long time doing the wrong things.

6. Another important item is training. Good training helps people do their job better and makes the job more enjoyable. It helps them to know that the job is being done right.

7. Then there is feedback. It's important to know how you are doing. How your work is perceived by management. Knowing that you're doing well is a motivator to keep doing well.

You can probably think of a few other important items.

Now we have a pretty good list of what will attract willing workers. It's our job as business owners to make sure we provide these things. It is also important that we make it blatantly obvious that we do provide these important elements.

Willing Workers Are Attracted To Great Employers

As business owners, we have to be attractive to prospective willing workers. We have to conduct ourselves professionally, dress properly, give people confidence that we know what we're doing.

The Ultimate Janitorial Success System provides every one of these important elements for your workers, including advancement for those that apply themselves and master these core business systems.

Your commitment to continuous growth and improvement provides the opportunity for everyone in your company to grow. A person starts as a helper making around $8 to $9 an hour. He can be promoted to a team leader making up to $10 or $12 per hour.

In time he can develop the skills necessary to become a unit manager making up to $12 to $15 per hour. From there, providing the company keeps growing, he could move into an executive position paying $50,000 to $75,000 per year. It's all part of the business growth system.

The Wrong Way

Now I want to talk about how not to have willing workers. One way is to subcontract your janitorial account to someone who will do the cleaning their own way, without the benefit of a system, without the benefit of supervision, without the benefit of training, without the benefit of good equipment and tools and without the benefit of the other elements that workers need to be successful.

Subcontracting your janitorial accounts in this way will lead to quality problems most, if not all of the time. We have seen this over and over for the last 40 years. It causes a large number of problems that are very easy to predict.

The first problem is supervision. When a worker is supervised you're ensuring that they are following your production system. If they are following your highly defined production system then 100% inspection of the work is not necessary because the production system will produce consistent high quality results.

Un-Supervised Sub-Contracting

When you use an unsupervised sub-contractor, they're not obligated to follow any system. Their obligation is only to clean the building, however they think is best. They are only responsible for the "result" rather than the "how".

They'll get paid the same amount, regardless of how long it takes to clean the building. Therefore their motivation is speed over quality. Many people will say their motivation is speed and quality but time and time again it's been proven that this motivation leads to poor quality.

If the unsupervised sub-contractor does a poor job, but the janitorial client doesn't complain, then they may be thinking that the client is happy. The people at the account may just be too busy to complain. They may think that it's not their job to complain. The account could be taking bids from other janitorial services because they don't want to complain. They may be tired of complaining.

Your Janitorial Accounts Are Valuable

If you lose the janitorial account, you will have lost a substantial investment. Getting janitorial accounts is quite expensive. The unsupervised sub-contractor, on the other hand, will have lost nothing, at least nothing of value.

He doesn't have a vested interested in the account. Because of this, if you use unsupervised sub-contractors you must inspect 100% of every account every time they clean. That's the only way you'll know that all of the work was completed according to the scope of work.

People try all kinds of incentive programs to make unsupervised sub-contracting work. But to maintain high quality using unsupervised sub-contractors requires 100% inspection, 100% of the time.

Inspecting Does Not Cause Quality

100% inspection 100% of the time isn't feasible. It cost too much. The reason people use unsupervised subcontractors in the first place was to save money, to avoid paying taxes and insurance.

When a janitorial account is sub-contracted the subcontractor is typically paid 35% to 40%. 100% inspection of your accounts can easily cost up to 20%. And that's providing that there is never any rework that has to be completed. Add the cost of rework and you're up to 30% for inspection and rework. There's just not enough money in a janitorial account to do all this.

Periodic Inspections?

The other option is to do periodic inspections. The problem with this is that the cleaning problems you find will be huge because they will have accumulated. And in many cases, by the time you discover the problem, there is significant damage to the janitorial client relationship.

Look at it from an unsupervised sub-contractors point of view. For just a moment pretend you're an unsupervised janitor. You do the work. You get paid. You do the work quickly you get the same money as if you do it slowly. You do a great job. Nobody checks. No problems. You do it fast and sloppy, nobody says anything different. You may talk to the boss who says; I haven't heard any complaints so I guess everything is OK. You do it even faster. No complaints. You still get paid the same money. You do a traffic vacuum instead of vacuuming the whole carpet. Nobody says anything. You still get paid the same money.

Quality Starts To Slide

In the restrooms you just wipe the top of the sinks and toilets. Nobody says anything. You still get paid the same money. You quit dusting every single time you clean. You just empty the trash. Nobody says anything. You still get paid the same money.

You do this for quite a while. You're making pretty good money for the time you're spending. Then the janitorial account complains. The boss comes out and looks at the building, sees the dust build up, sees the bases of the toilets, sees the cobwebs, sees the dirt built up along the edges and corners. Then the boss tells you to clean it all up.

The boss wants you to do ten times more work than you have been doing and he wants it done all at once. And he wants you to do it for - you guessed it - the same money you have been receiving. Now what are the chances of getting someone to do even twice as much work for the same money? I'd say slim to none.

And this happens time after time with the excuse that you just can't find good workers. The problem wasn't the worker. The problem was the system. The system will give the same results time after time - Good work at first - Quality slowly deteriorating - Boss gives an ultimatum to shape up the building or ship out - Old sub-contractor out. - New sub-contractor in - Same process - Same results. After a few cycles the account will be lost because of inconsistent service.

Who's Really To Blame?

One of the problems that we'll talk more about later is blaming the results of the system on the workers. When you do this, there is no hope for improvement. You have to look at what the production system is producing. If it's unacceptable then change the system.

It must operate just like a cookie cutter producing identical results every time - it must be reliable. The results must be sure and certain. This can be a very profitable and a very safe business when you follow a proven system that produces predictable results.

The system calls for workers to be compensated by the hour, not by the job. Their job is to produce quality with as few defects as possible. They're required to do their best every day, every clean. No one will ask them to do twice as much work tomorrow as they did today for the same money. No one will pay them for work they pretended to do but didn't because they decided they could get away with not doing it.

As we said in the beginning, to get good workers, you have to be a good employer.

Things To Remember:

- Good cleaning personnel are attracted to great employers.

- Great employers give their personnel all of the elements they need in order for them to be great.

- Unsupervised subcontracting doesn't work.

- Janitorial Accounts are valuable.

- Inspection does not cause quality.

- The business owner is the one accountable for the quality of services provided by their business.

GLEN SPRINGFIELD

Chapter 8

TOOLS & SUPPLY STRATEGY

The next item on our UJSS list of ingredients is your equipment and supply strategy.

Our cleaning strategy is based on two or three-man cleaning teams. You will learn more about that a little later.

We'll start by looking at the set of tools and products that are used by a Team Helper also called a General Cleaning Specialist.

Below is a list of the equipment and supplies used by the General Cleaning Specialist in my business.

General Cleaning Specialist – Team Helpers Tools and Products:

1. Super H2O2 Concentrate
2. ECloths
3. ECloth container with lid
4. Micro-Fiber Polish Cloths
5. Speed Trowel

6. Tool Belt System with 2 Unger Pouches
7. Tool / Utility Bucket
8. Plastic Putty Knife/Scraper
9. White Pad
10. Green Pad
11. 12" Professional Squeegee
12. Micro Fiber Wave Duster
13. Trash Barrel on Wheels
14. Trash Barrel Caddy
15. Heavy Duty Cleaner
16. Mineral Shock
17. Disinfectant
18. Razor Scraper
19. Detail Brush
20. Rubber Gloves
21. Bowl Mop
22. Red and Green Spray Bottle

A Team Helper is supervised by a Team Leader who also has a set of products, tools and duties. Team Leaders are also called VAC Specialist.

Below is a list of the supplies and equipment used by the VAC specialist.

Team Leader – VAC Specialist Tools

1. HEPA Backpack Vacuum with Tools
2. Tool Bucket

3. Tool Belt With One Unger Pouch
4. Carpet Spotter and Brush Belt System
5. Hard Floor Tools
6. Micro-Fiber Mop Bucket with lid
7. Micro-Fiber Mop Frame
8. Micro-Fiber Mop Heads
9. Micro-Fiber Dust Mop (Complete)

Good Tools Save More Money Than They Cost

Good tools save money in the long run. They save time and they improve quality. Shoddy work often begins with shoddy tools.

There isn't room in this manuscript to explain the purpose of each tool and give instructions on how each one is used.

The thing to keep in mind is that good workers need good tools to do good work.

Another thing to remember is that labor is and always will be the largest expense in the janitorial business. In almost all cases, great tools pay for themselves quickly in the form of saved labor.

Your Equipment and Supply Strategy

Now let's talk about your strategy for the distribution and maintenance of supplies and equipment.

There are 3 basic strategies being used in the industry today for the distribution and maintenance of cleaning supplies and equipment. Two of these strategies produce bad results. One produces good results. I'll give you the two bad strategies first. Then I'll give you the best strategy along with the reasons why it's the best strategy.

Wrong Way #1

Wrong way number one is to put a set of equipment and supplies in each account, or on each floor of an account. One set for each employee in large buildings. This is the way the whole industry worked for many years. You let the workers maintain the equipment and refill bottles from a supply kept at each building or in each janitorial closet in large buildings.

When supplies run low, the worker lets the supervisor know and the supervisor will bring additional supplies. If a tool or piece of equipment fails, the supervisor brings a replacement and takes the broken equipment in for repair. That's wrong way number one.

Wrong Way #2

Wrong way number two is similar to number one except you give one set of equipment and supplies to each Team Leader of a two man team, instead of to each building or each worker. This cuts down on the amount of equipment needed because the team leader takes the equipment from building to building on route work, and on large buildings one set of equipment serves two workers. The Team Leader is responsible for maintaining the equipment refilling the bottles and pretreating cloths and mop pads from his stock. When he runs out, he gets more from his unit manager.

The main thing wrong with these two strategies is the results. Chemical and product waste will be very high. Equipment maintenance will be poor or non-existent. The equipment will be abused and very soon it will be trashed beyond recognition. It will be unpresentable and in many cases, not working well. Remember that one of the things that employees want and need are good tools to work with.

The Way That Works Every Time

The right way is to issue a full and complete set of equipment and supplies to each Team Leader, each evening when they come to work. The equipment should be perfectly clean and checked out before the team leaders arrive for work. All spray bottles should be filled and tested.

Two dozen microfiber cleaning cloths should be counted out; One, two, three, four, five six.

At the end of the shift the team leader should turn everything in. The vacuum should be emptied and wiped down, inside and out, before it's turned in. The microfiber cleaning cloths should be counted as they are turned in -two dozen cloths out, two dozen cloths in.

Lost microfiber cleaning cloths cost the team a dollar each. Damage to equipment from abuse is charged to the team. The mop bucket was clean when it was checked out, it should be wiped out and clean when it is checked in.

Setup For The Next Work Day

Before the next evening the microfiber cleaning cloths and mop pads will be laundered, the spray bottles will be tested; all vacuums will be checked out and tested. This system reduces the variation in quality that comes from poorly cared for equipment, poor maintenance and the lack of proper supplies.

Following this program will reduce chemical usage by 500%. It will prolong the life of your equipment and increase the life of your microfiber cleaning cloths by 1000%. It's the only way to ensure that everyone has everything they need to follow the production system every time they clean. This strategy works every time. Everything else is a gamble. And the success of your business is not something you want to gamble on.

Things To Remember:

- Define what janitorial tools and products you are going to use.

- Eliminate all variation in tools, equipment and cleaning supplies from your production system.

- There are many strategies for managing janitorial tools and supplies that do not work.

- The quality and condition of janitorial cleaning tools and supplies greatly affect the quality of the work done and the time it take to do the work.

- Your business system must take accountability for maintaining all cleaning tools, equipment and supplies.

- A good janitorial cleaning tool and supply strategy will enhance work quality and reduce labor costs.

- An ineffective tool and supply strategy will cost more in the long run.

Chapter 9

SUPERVISION & QUALITY CONTROL

The next ingredient on the list is supervision. Supervision is an important part of the production system. To give you an easy example of why it's important, think about a General Motors Cadillac factory.

As you may know Cadillac won the Malcom Baldric award for quality several years ago. So, you can say they produce pretty good quality in their factories. They have pretty good employees doing pretty good work.

But, what would happen if they suddenly fired all of the supervisors and managers. What would happen to the quality of the product then? No supervisors, no supervision. Everyone just does their job the way they think they are supposed to. Which way would the quality go? Obviously the quality would go down - but why?

Why Would Quality Decrease?

You have the very same workers doing the very same jobs. Is it because the workers are bad workers? Or that they're bad people? Is it because they're lazy? No. It's because supervision is an important part of the production system.

Some people think that a supervisor's job is to inspect work and then correct the people who are responsible forcing them to do a better job. Nothing could be further from the truth.

Inspecting Never Causes Quality!

Inspecting can identify poor quality, but inspecting a finished job never causes quality in that job. It's too late. The job is finished. Following a good production system without variation causes consistent quality while the work is being done.

The job of a supervisor is to make it easy for a worker to do their job. A supervisor is there to make sure the workers are following the production system. When he finds deviation from the system, his job is to instruct, train and demonstrate correct methods.

Coaching

Assuming he has willing workers who want their job, who want to do their best and who are committed to continuous improvement, a supervisor's job is that of a teacher or coach.

A supervisor doesn't have time to inspect everything that a team does. He will regularly check on a team to make sure they are following the production system without unwanted variation.

The workers never know when they'll be checked. It shouldn't matter. They should know that the supervisor is there to help them do their job better, not to catch them doing something wrong and get them in trouble.

Think of a good coach working with an athlete. Just like a good coach, a good supervisor helps good employees perform better.

Supervision is a critical part of the system.

Here's How You Keep Your Janitorial Accounts Loyal and Happy Forever

TQM stands for Total Quality Management. TQM is a quality management process and philosophy developed by W. Edward Deming based on strict system control plus incremental improvement.

Success in the janitorial business is completely dependent on the quality and efficiency of the services delivered.

Poor Or Marginal Service Will Always Lose Money And Customers.

Keeping your customers happy is absolutely necessary to janitorial success! Your customer retention will be determined by the quality and the consistency of the service you provide!

This may seem so obvious that it doesn't even need to be stated but it does. People fall out of the janitorial business all of the time because the services they provide do not satisfy their customers.

They get fired and then they think it is some stroke of bad luck or the world is against them when actually it was only poor quality or poor consistency in the services they provided.

It is very common for someone in the janitorial business to pay someone else to clean their accounts and do absolutely no inspections or quality control. They simply believe in their deluded imagination that the people they are paying to clean are actually performing the cleaning as well as they did when they were performing the cleaning processes themselves.

They become surprised when they find how poorly their own workers were performing their duties. Unfortunately, by the time they find out it is too late to save the customer.

To manage quality, you can't wait until a customer complains. You have to deploy a quality management strategy before cleaning problems arise to prevent poor quality from ever getting past your systems and getting to your janitorial clients.

Here Are 7 Keys To Quality Management:

- Commit to quality
- Only hire and keep willing workers
- Have a strict cleaning system
- Provide easy to follow training
- Insist on strict system compliance
- Inspect what you expect
- Don't tolerate system resistant people

Now I will add a comment or two about each of these points.

Commit To Quality.

Quality doesn't happen by accident. It happens by intention and by the implementation of a plan that will bring about quality. If you are not totally committed to quality then you won't even notice all of the clues that are right in front of your nose, in plain sight that would expose the possibility or even probability of poor quality.

Poor Quality is an expensive destroyer of service businesses. You can't afford it so you have to make sure you keep it out of your business. That will only happen if you are totally committed to quality.

Only Hire and Keep Willing Workers.

When Dr. Deming wrote the book on Total Quality Management,

he introduced the term "willing worker". A willing worker is someone who wants to be there, wants to do the work and wants to do the work well. Willing workers can be trained and counted on to do their jobs without micro management.

All too often janitorial positions are occupied by people who really don't want to be there, they don't really want to do the work and they don't really care about quality. Those people are often relatives of the business owner who need the money but don't really want to do the work. They kill janitorial businesses.

I am grateful for these people because they are so common they give us a steady supply of new clients who are tired of paying for a level of service they aren't receiving.

Have A Strict Cleaning System.

The biggest secret to managing quality is systematization. McDonald's first mastered systemization in the fast food market. Their efficiency and their ability to deliver consistent value across the country and around the world put almost all of the mom and pop hamburger stands out of business.

The thing that causes poor quality is "variation". Variation in tools, variation in products, variation in processes all cause variation in results. The goal in managing quality is to eliminate variation in tools, products and processes so that you eliminate variation in cleaning results.

When you eliminate variation then you are managing quality.

Provide Easy To Follow Training

In order to successfully eliminate variation, you have to provide easy to learn training. It should be noted that training is only effective for people who want to learn your system. These are the willing workers we referred to earlier.

A common rookie mistake is to try to teach too much of the system at one time. It is better to train new personnel in one aspect of the system, let the individual get some experience and master that aspect of the business before training them in additional aspects of the business.

In other words, McDonalds doesn't take a brand new employee and run through – this is how we make fries, this is how we clean tables, this is how we make Big Macs, this is how we clean restrooms, this is how we run a cash register, this is how we input orders, this is how we clean glass – Now go make fries. That would be more training than a new employee could remember or put to use. They would just be confused and they probably couldn't do anything right.

But, teach them one thing at a time, let them master each procedure before they learn a new procedure and very soon they will have mastered all of the processes and can perform them within the system.

In the janitorial business the same concept can be applied by teaching someone to do general office cleaning – pulling trash, dusting and minor surface cleaning. Later they can learn restroom cleaning, Later still, they can learn how to mop and vacuum, fill restroom supplies, etc.

Insist On Strict System Compliance

Everyone has opinions on the best way to clean. Everyone has an opinion on the best way to make the best hamburger too. McDonalds doesn't care about their employees opinions of their production methods or products and neither should you. Before you can refine a system you must eliminate variation from the system so the system can be evaluated.

System deviation can kill your business so don't tolerate it.

McDonalds doesn't try to make hamburgers like Burger King. Burger King doesn't try to make hamburgers like McDonalds. Each has their own system. Their systems are different and produce different products. But both products are very consistent and therefore very successful.

Learn from these and a thousand other successful businesses. Insist on strict system compliance.

Inspect What You Expect.

There is a show on TV where a restaurant turnaround specialist goes into a restaurant and installs hidden cameras to monitor what is really going on when no one is looking. The restaurant owners are appalled to discover the truth about their own personnel.

Don't make the mistake of taking for granted that your workers are doing what they are supposed to be doing, the way they are supposed to be doing it.

Workers need feedback on their work so their work gets better and not worse. If you aren't looking, work standards will deteriorate quickly and you will lose money and accounts.

Inspect what you expect. The best way to inspect is to inspect while the work is being done so that you are observing the process. It is easy to tell very quickly if someone is functioning within your production system or if they are off track.

Don't Tolerate System Resistant People

If you are spot checking work while the work is being done then you will find system deviation. That deviation will be the result of one of two things. The individual either doesn't understand the production system or they are system resistant.

If personnel do not understand the production system then they can be retrained. If they are system resistant then all of the training in the world will not help. System resistant people must be eliminated from your company if you are going to eliminate variation and manage quality.

System resistant personnel can't be fixed. They are passive-resistant. They will agree to follow the system, but then you will find that they aren't following the system. They will always have an excuse. Don't tolerate this. Variation will kill your quality and kill your business. Get rid of system resistant people ASAP.

If you follow these simple guidelines then you will have a head start on managing the quality control aspect of your business. As a matter of fact, you will outperform 99.9% of your competition.

Things To Remember:

There are seven keys to Quality Management that will make your business more effective, easier to manage, more profitable and more fun.

- Commit to quality
- Hire and keep only willing workers
- Have a strict cleaning system
- Provide easy to follow training
- Insist on strict system compliance
- Inspect what you expect
- Don't tolerate system resistant people

Chapter 10

STRATEGIC EXPANSION

Your growth strategy must be built on a solid foundation of good values and beliefs. It is important that you write down and make public your business values and beliefs. These declarations are the foundation upon which your business will be built. Your company's public proclamation of its fundamental values and beliefs can make or break your company. Here's why.

Every company has a set of values and beliefs about itself, its customers, its vendors and its employees whether they know it or not. The company's philosophy is communicated through the way they interact with their customers, their suppliers and their employees. It's the very personality of the company.

It's especially apparent in the way personnel are managed and the way workers interact with each other. It's also demonstrated in the level of quality that is delivered to the market place.

Too often company values and beliefs are developed by chance, just through the natural evolution of relationships and don't represent what management originally intended.

The vision and principles of a company should come from the top and be strictly enforced on all levels. It guides the day to day decisions and the attitudes of management and holds the company to its very purpose.

Below is a Sample Value and Belief Statement. You should write your own; however this will give you an idea about the types of things that are addressed by these important declarations.

Sample Company Value and Belief Statements

Administration:

"World Class" is the key phrase throughout the Company and building a team is of primary importance. Everyone is expected to do their personal best at all times. We will tolerate nothing less. Each person is accountable for their own results, good and bad. We treat each other with dignity and respect. We strive to make each other look good. We are good neighbors to our customers, our co-workers, and our environment.

Personnel:

We hire only those people who share a commitment to world class performance and take pride in their work. We provide world class training. We expect world class work. We focus on building people as well as building a team. We work as a team while acknowledging the individual contributions responsible for team results.

Marketing:

We deal with integrity, promise only what we can deliver, and go the extra mile to keep the customer happy. Our pricing accurately reflects a value to the customer. We will not ask the customer to pay for our mistakes.

Quality:

World class quality is demonstrated in our commitment to always do our best and to always be our best. We do not tolerate poor work. We take pride in our personal and professional appearance. It shows in everything we do. From our dress code and personal grooming to the way we take care of our equipment and supplies. These details are just part of the consistent high quality service we are proud of. We maintain a level of quality that produces first rate references and referrals. We work hard to always provide world class quality knowing that it is easier to build on a good reputation than it is to repair a bad one.

Communication:

We make it easy for our customers and co-workers to communicate with us. We are available. We listen carefully. We put ourselves in the other person's shoes. We make no excuses or assumptions. We are problem solvers. We maintain an optimistic attitude. We are positive and resourceful.

Your Value and Belief Statements

As you can see, the philosophy of your company is what guides your business decisions and the decisions of those that work for you. You have to make your philosophy known and followed throughout your company or it will be of little effect.

As we said before, every company has a philosophy whether they know it or not. You can do business with a company for a very short period of time and have a good idea of the philosophy that drives the company.

Your staff will only take this seriously when you write down your philosophy and clearly communicate to everyone in your company that this is the way we are and this is the way we act. Then you must model correct behavior and enforce compliance on every level. Then you'll you have control of your company and control of your company's future.

Long Term Staffing Plan

Next, I will explain the basic growth plan. The following pages describe the positions found in a successful janitorial company. When you begin your business, you're a company of one, and you will fill all these positions. You have one big job. Take a moment to review each position and the job description. You will need to have a basic understanding of each position to get the big picture of how to build a business that will get you from where you are to where you want to be.

The top position in the company is the General Manager. The general manager is responsible for the company providing world class service to all customers and maintaining a high level of customer satisfaction. That means the buck stops here.

Below is a Sample Job Description for a General Manager

Position: General Manager / Owner

Manages: Supervisors and Administrative Staff

Basic Function:

Plan, organize, control and direct the activities of the Company to achieve specific profit, sales and return on investment objectives while providing world-class service to all customers and maintaining a high level of customer satisfaction.

Major Responsibilities:

1. Formulate company objectives and policies.
2. Guide and direct staff in the identification of objectives and the preparation of plans and programs.

3. Prepare and supervise the implementation of business plans.

4. Continually analyze company performance against objectives and budget and take corrective action when deviation occurs.

5. Develop and train management personnel and review and appraise their performance.

6. Approve expenditures.

7. Interpret and insure the carrying out established policies, methods and procedures. Make recommendations concerning new or improved methods.

8. Establish and maintain effective and continuing relationships with business and community leaders.

9. Perform other duties as necessary for the overall success of the business.

The next position is Warehouse Supervisor. This position is responsible for maintaining all equipment, refilling bottles, pretreating cloths and mop pads, laundering microfiber cleaning cloths and maintaining inventory records.

The next job is the Warehouse Supervisor. A sample job description is below.

Position: Warehouse Supervisor

Reports To: General Manager

Basic Function:

Receives, dispenses, and accounts for supplies and equipment. Repairs and maintains equipment.

Major Responsibilities:

1. Receives shipments of supplies and materials; verifies shipment against bill of lading, places supplies in prearranged space in the warehouse.

2. Refills spray bottles, oversees cleaning of uniforms, and launders cleaning cloths and mop pads daily to insure timely, efficient processing of supply and material requests prior to the beginning of each shift.

3. Conducts periodic and specific inventories to maintain required level of supplies and equipment; submits requests for restocking to Bookkeeping Supervisor.

4. Inspects, cleans and maintains a variety of floor machines, vacuums, sweepers and other building maintenance equipment. Performs repairs such as replacing plugs, cables and other components.

5. Maintains equipment records and warranty information.

6. Makes recommendations concerning replacement of worn out equipment.

7. Performs other duties as assigned by the General Manager.

The next position is Bookkeeper / Human Resources. This person is responsible for personnel records, hiring, firing, processing payroll, purchasing equipment and supplies to maintain proper inventories.

A Sample Job Description for that job is below:

Position: Bookkeeper / Human Resource Manager

Reports To: General Manager

Basic Function:

Prepares and maintains records relating to the firm's financial activities. Interprets and implements approved personnel policies and procedures, develops and recommends local policies as required. Provides support in the areas of employment compensation, benefits, safety, federal compliance and training and supervises payroll. Responsible for all Company purchasing requirements.

Major Responsibilities:

1. Maintains the general & subsidiary ledgers, journals and supporting schedules. Prepares journal entries. Records and processes accounts receivable & payable. Maintains & reconciles bank accounts and petty cash.

2. Assists in preparing annual budget and in analyzing monthly financial results. Maintains cost controls; prepares labor distribution reports and periodic cost reports as required by General Manager.

3. Prepares various insurance payments and sales tax returns, and maintains records. Records claims for health insurance. Prepare reports on pension, insurance, bonds, loans, employment verification, EEO, safety, etc.

4. Establishes required inventory controls to include vehicles, equipment and expendable supply and inventory records. Prepares and/or supervises the preparation of purchase orders and the maintenance of purchase records.

5. Recruit, test, hire and orients non-exempt hourly personnel. Maintain personnel records. Develop and supervise Human Resource procedures. Implement established programs in safety and equal opportunity.

6. Processes executive & regular payroll time records; calls in to Contract Payroll Service at appointed day/time. Receives

payroll checks for signature and distribution to appropriate personnel.

7. Performs other duties as assigned by General Manager.

The next position is Supervisor. A Supervisor organizes teams, assigns routes and duties, checks out and in all supplies and equipment, inspects the work of teams making adjustments as necessary to insure all work is completed properly.

A Sample Job Description for that position is below:

Position: Unit Manager

Reports To: General Manager

Supervises: Team Leaders (General and Utility)

Basic Function:

Coordinates and supervises the servicing of assigned accounts to conform to direct cost budgets, quality standards, and customer satisfaction. Coordinates the activities of new job start-ups. Provides assistance to the General Manager in accomplishing special projects.

Major Responsibilities:

1. Plan and organize the operations of the Teams. Encompasses reviewing and controlling manpower and supply costs for assigned accounts to assure conformance with budgetary standards and operational practices; maintaining performance records for Owner's monthly review; scheduling personnel and the Team's workload & route on a weekly basis; reallocating work as required because of personnel shortage or special requirements; and identifying and developing supervisory potential within the crews.

2. Scheduling and coordinating of periodic work; evaluating the quantity of work on a weekly basis; and maintaining records of work completed.

3. Coordinate new job start-ups in accordance with company procedure. This involves coordination with Team Leader to insure an understanding of the requirements of the new job (accomplished on site); that the proper supplies and equipment are on site when job starts; that the requisite numbers and types of personnel are on site when job starts; that adequate work schedules and work plan have been prepared prior to starting; communication during first week of work to insure job is conforming to plans; and reporting "after action" and "lessons learned."

4. Responsible for check-out and check-in of all equipment and supplies each evening. Approves requests for additional supplies and equipment.

5. Reviews and certifies labor time sheets prior to submission.

6. Recommends actions for hiring, disciplining, promoting and discharging of employees.

7. Responsible for resolving day-to-day operations problems at his/her teams.

8. Continually evaluates methods, procedures and materials for purposes of improving performance and reducing cost of operation.

9. Performs any and all other duties assigned by General Manager.

As you can see a Unit Manager has a long job description with many duties and responsibilities. The supervisor answers directly to the General Manager. This position carries more responsibility than any other except the General Manager.

The next position is a Utility Team Leader. A Utility Team Leader does the high speed buffing, adds floor finish, and does the periodic strip and refinishing, carpet cleaning plus a few other periodic duties that aren't covered by the General Cleaning Teams.

A Sample Job Description for that position is below:

Position: Team Leader / Utility

Reports To: Unit Manager

Supervises: Team Helper / Utility

Basic Function:

Responsible for periodic and/or routine tasks as assigned by Team Supervisor. Directs, supervises and inspects the work of Team Helper to insure world-class service is provided to every customer. Performs cleaning and maintenance tasks.

Major Responsibilities:

1. Performs tasks of mopping, high-speed buffing, adding floor finish, stripping and refinishing, carpet cleaning plus other periodic duties as required. Works extra time to complete work of absent employees if necessary.

2. Is responsible for insuring that every job performed satisfies specifications and customer quality expectations.

3. Indoctrinates and trains new cleaning personnel. Makes recommendations concerning compensation adjustments.

4. Requisitions and is accountable for necessary equipment and supplies.

5. Continually evaluates methods, procedures and materials for purposes of suggesting ways for improving performance and reducing cost of operation.
6. Takes immediate action on routine complaints pertaining to accounts.
7. Reviews and certifies labor time sheets prior to submission.
8. Performs such other duties as assigned by the Unit Manager.

The next position is the Utility Team Helper. This person works with the Utility Team Leader, helping him in those same duties.

A Sample Job Description for that position is below:

Position Title: Team Helper/Utility

Reports To: Team Leader/Utility

Basic Function:

Performs janitorial tasks.

Major Responsibilities:

1. Assists Team Leader with cleaning tasks such as mopping, high-speed buffing, adding floor finish, stripping and refinishing, carpet cleaning plus other periodic duties as assigned. Operates a variety of building maintenance equipment.
2. In addition to work tasks, the Team Helper/Utility is required to report requests for equipment and supplies; hours worked; building condition and problems.
3. Takes corrective action as directed by the Team Leader.
4. Performs other related duties as assigned by the Team Leader.

Next is the General Team Leader. The General Team Leader's duties are to vacuum floors, spot mop where needed, spot clean carpet where needed, stock restrooms with supplies, plus inspect the work of his helper to ensure all work is completed properly.

A Sample Job Description for that position is below:

Position: Team Leader / General

Reports To: Unit Manager

Supervises: Team Helper / General

Basic Function:

Responsible for several buildings in an assigned area of operation. Directs, supervises and inspects the work of Team Helper to insure world-class service is provided every customer. Performs janitorial tasks.

Major Responsibilities:

1. Performs basic cleaning tasks of vacuuming, spot mopping, spot cleaning carpets, and restocking restrooms. Works extra time to complete work of absent employees if necessary.

2. During cleaning, Team Leader is responsible for inspecting each account to insure that the work performed satisfies cleaning specifications and customer quality expectations.

3. Indoctrinates and trains new cleaning personnel. Makes recommendations covering salary adjustment.

4. Requisitions and is accountable for necessary equipment and supplies for his/her route.

5. Continually evaluates methods, procedures and materials for purposes of suggesting ways for improving performance and reducing cost of operation.

6. Takes immediate action on routine complaints pertaining to accounts.

7. Reviews and certifies labor time sheets prior to submission.

8. Performs such other duties as assigned by the Unit Manager.

Last is the General Team Helper. The General Team Helper's duties are to empty trash, clean ashtrays and horizontal surfaces, dust furniture and equipment, clean and sanitize restrooms.

A Sample Job Description for that position is below:

Position Title: Team Helper/General

Reports To: Team Leader/General

Basic Function:

Performs janitorial tasks.

Major Responsibilities:

1. Performs basic cleaning tasks of trash collection & removal, clean ashtrays, damp wiping horizontal surfaces, dusting furniture & equipment, and restroom sanitization.

2. In addition to work tasks, the Team Helper/General is required to report requests for equipment and supplies; hours worked; building condition and problems.

3. Takes corrective action as directed by the Team Leader.

4. Performs other related duties as assigned by the Team Leader.

Start Small - Do It All!

From the team that does the general cleaning, to the team that does the utility work, to the Unit Manager, to purchasing, personnel and payroll, to equipment maintenance and supply inventory, to the general manager. You occupy all of these positions when you first begin.

As a one person company, you'll be able to do approximately $2,500 per month in about 20 hours a week. Of course this is after you've had a little experience and you've mastered your highly efficient cleaning system. If you can devote full-time to your business, you can clean approximately $4,000 to $5,000 per month by yourself in a 40 hour week.

Even as a one person company, you're using the same cleaning strategy as if you were a two man team. First, you do the Team Helper's job: empty trash, clean ashtrays and horizontal surfaces, dust furniture and equipment, clean and sanitize restrooms.

After you've completed the Team Helper's duties, you "change hats" and do the Team Leader's duties. They are: vacuum floors, spot mop where needed, spot clean carpet where needed, stock restrooms with supplies plus inspect the work of the helper to insure all the work is completed properly.

Your third "hat" will be doing the work of the utility crew: high speed buffing, adding floor finish, stripping and refinishing. The next step is to begin using others to do the cleaning.

So, How Do You Find Great Cleaning Staff?

To attract and keep great cleaning staff you need 3 things.

1. You need an entry level position where people can start. This position must not require great skill or experience. This position is an entry level position where people can demonstrate their work ethics, their dedication to the

company, the company's systems and values. This position must be completely supervised.

2. You need a higher position that good workers can aspire to and grow into where they can assume more responsibility and make more money.

3. You need a feedback loop that recognizes and rewards good behavior.

In a profitable cleaning team, the entry level position is called a General Cleaning Specialist. This person will remove trash, dust and clean surfaces in a single pass through the cleanable area.

This person is supervised by the Team Leader who vacuums the floors while inspecting the work of the General Cleaning Specialist. A General Cleaning Specialist can be trained in a few minutes and develop both skill and speed on the job.

Since General Cleaning Specialist are supervised by the Team Leader, any mistakes or omissions can be corrected before they can be seen or experienced by a customer.

It is important that the Team Leader and the General Cleaning Specialist are not related in any way. They can't be relatives, neighbors or have any other relationship where special treatment or consideration might be expected.

They both need to be "willing workers" with independent relationships with the company. That way, if a General Cleaning Specialist is not a good fit for the job, they can be easily replaced without affecting other workers.

Building profitable, system compliant cleaning teams is like digging for gold. You have to go through a lot of dirt. The key is, you don't keep the dirt.

A lot of people begin a job at McDonald's who don't last a week. That's OK because since their work was supervised, any flaws or errors they made didn't affect the McDonald's customer experience or the consistency of their products.

Even though some new McDonald's employees don't last a week, some do. Some go on to become shift managers, assistant managers and even store managers. There is a lot of turnover at the bottom but McDonald's is able to deliver the most consistent customer experience in Fast Food with very low paid staff.

When Janitorial Services use these same principles, they will also deliver a consistent customer experience at a higher than normal profit.

Basic Growth Plan

After you've perfected and mastered your cleaning "System", the next step in building your business is to hire a helper.

The person that you hire will work closely with you. They'll be the Team Helper and you'll be the Team Leader. You'll inspect all the work they do every night while you carry out the Team Leader duties.

You can expect to go through a few people before you find an individual that becomes a good Helper. The important thing is to determine if the person you hired will help you get to where you want to be or whether they will slow you down. You can't fix unwilling workers. Don't try. Once you have determined that and individual is not a "willing worker" you must terminate that relationship and replace them with a willing worker.

With experience, you will get better and better at selecting willing workers. You will know what to look for and develop questions to ask that will help you in your selection decisions.

You'll pay a Team Helper about $8 to $9 per hour. With you leading a two person team, you should be able to clean up to approximately $8,000 to $9,000 per month working a standard 40 hour week.

A 3 Person Company

When you have a helper that has demonstrated the skills and responsibilities to be a Team Leader, you can promote him to a Team Leader position and hire a Helper to work with them. As a Team Leader they will earn about $10.00 to $12.00 per hour.

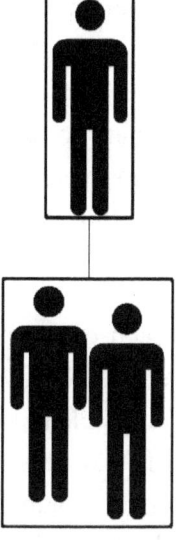

In this 3 person configuration, you can build up to approximately $12,000 to $13,500 per month. The 2 person team will do the same $8,000 to $9,000 per month in accounts and you'll clean $4,000 to $4,500 in accounts yourself while you periodically check on your team to make sure they're following the production system without variation.

A 4 Person Company

The next step is to hire a helper to work with you. A four person company can clean up to $16,000 to $18,000 per month with everyone working a standard 40 hour week.

A 5 Person Company

When one of the Helpers has demonstrated that they are ready, you can promote them to a Team Leader and hire another Helper. As a five person company, you can clean up to $20,000 per month with everyone working a standard 40 hour week.

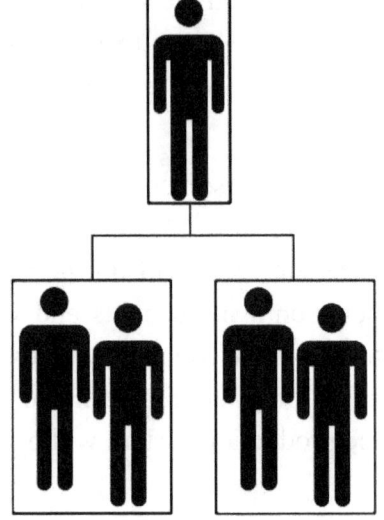

Each of your teams will be doing up to $8,000 to $9,000 each and you'll clean a few thousand dollars of business yourself while you check each team to make sure they're following the production system.

A 6 Person Company

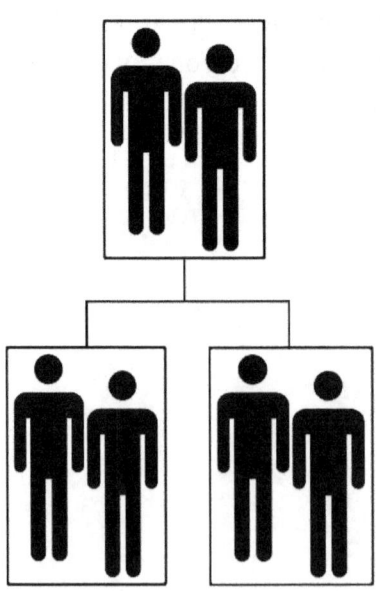

The next step is to hire another Helper to work with you. As a 6-person company, you can clean up to $24,000 per month with everyone working a standard 40-hour week.

A 7 Person Company

The next step is to promote your very best Helper to a Team Leader position and hire another Helper. A 7 man company can clean up to $27,000 per month.

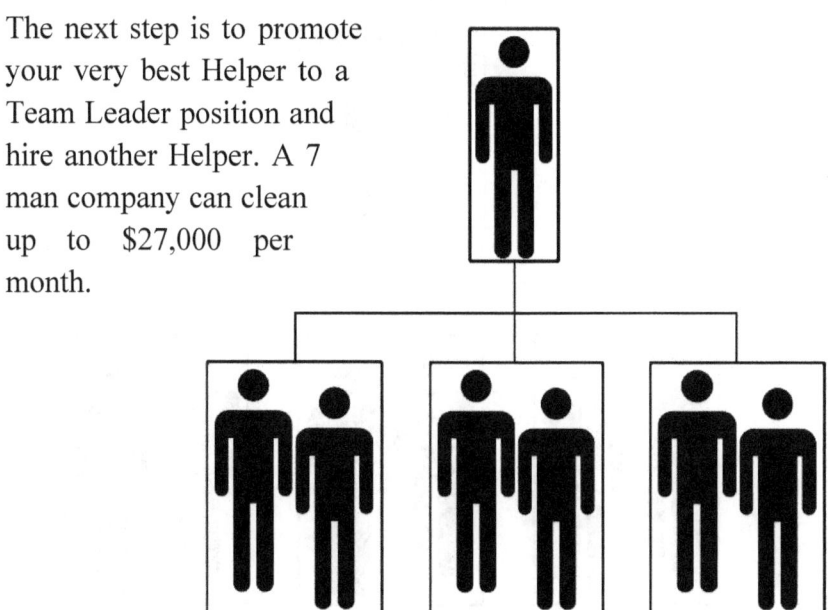

You would do the utility work, like buffing and adding floor finish to floors, yourself, while you checked on each team to make sure everyone has everything they need and are following the production system.

An 8 Person Company

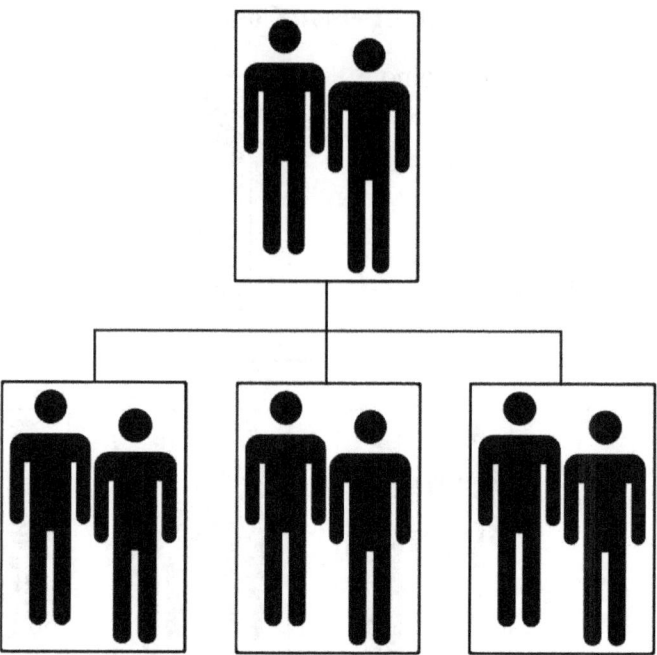

The next step is to hire another Helper. An 8 person company can clean up to $32,000 per month with everyone working a standard 40 hour week. Now you are beginning to have a nice size business.

Picture this. Everyone comes to work at about 5:30 in the afternoon. All the Team Leaders know their routes. You hand out the keys, the alarm codes, the equipment and supplies to each Team Leader. You assign a Helper to work with each Team Leader.

You'll change the Helper assignments every few nights for a couple of reasons. First, you want every Helper to become familiar with all the routes. This helps in the transition when someone is promoted to a Team Leader position.

Second, you want Helpers to work with different Team Leaders to keep everyone following the production system. If 2 people work together too often, they get comfortable with each other and can begin to get sloppy in their work.

Third, you want every Helper to work with the "best" Team Leader as well as the "not as great" Team Leader to learn the differences between the two and so no one Helper will be more affected by the difference in leadership.

Fourth, you want every helper to have the opportunity to work directly with you and learn how to do the utility work.

When your company gets to this size, several things get easier for you. If a helper calls in sick or doesn't show up, you just work without a helper that night. If 2 helpers call in sick, you can work with a Team Leader yourself. If 3 helpers call in sick, you can have one Team Leader work alone and assign a few of their buildings to the other teams.

When your company is this size, a third of your people can fail to show up and you will still get your routes cleaned without much inconvenience or overtime.

If you get sick or want to leave town for a few days, you can have your best Team Leader fill in for you as Supervisor. You wouldn't want to be gone too long, but if everyone is trained to follow the system, it would be safe for you to be gone for a few days or a long weekend.

A 9 Person Company

The next step is to promote your best Helper to a Team Leader position and hire another Helper. Notice that everyone you hire is started at the Helper position. This is important because if the people you hire know that they are working for a growing company, and that they can advance within the company, it will add to their job satisfaction, their stability and their longevity with the company.

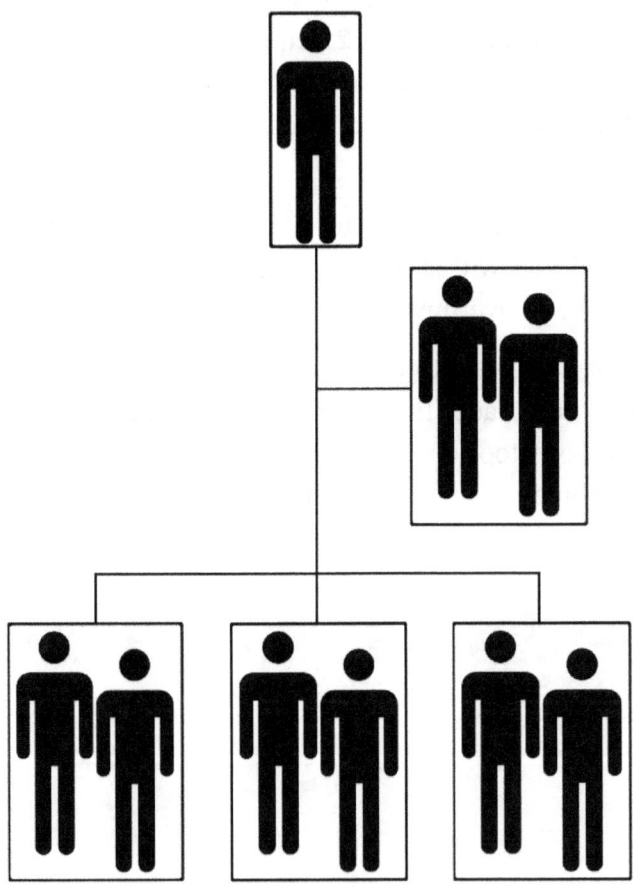

This time you also promoted someone to be a Utility Team Leader. A 9 person company can easily clean up to $36,000 per month.

A 10 Person Company

The next step is to make your Utility Team Leader a general Team Leader. You will take over the utility Team Leader's duties and hire another Helper.

Now you have a 10 man company. A 10 man full time company can clean up to $40,000 per month.

An 11 Person Company

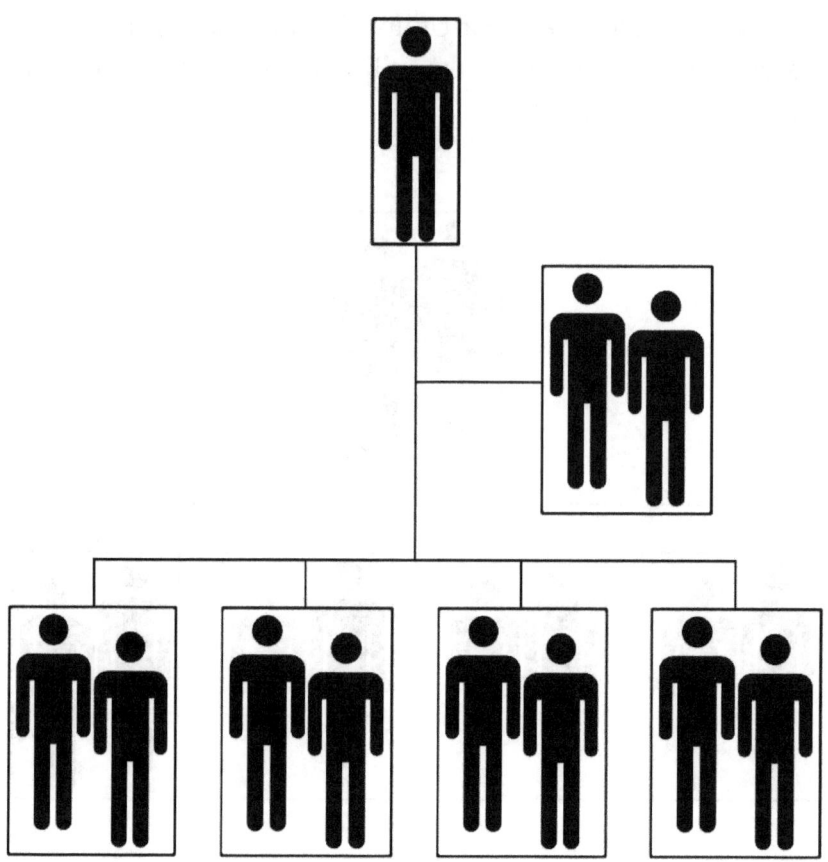

The next step is to promote a new utility Team Leader and hire a new Helper. An 11 person company can clean up to $43,000 per month.

A 12 Person Company

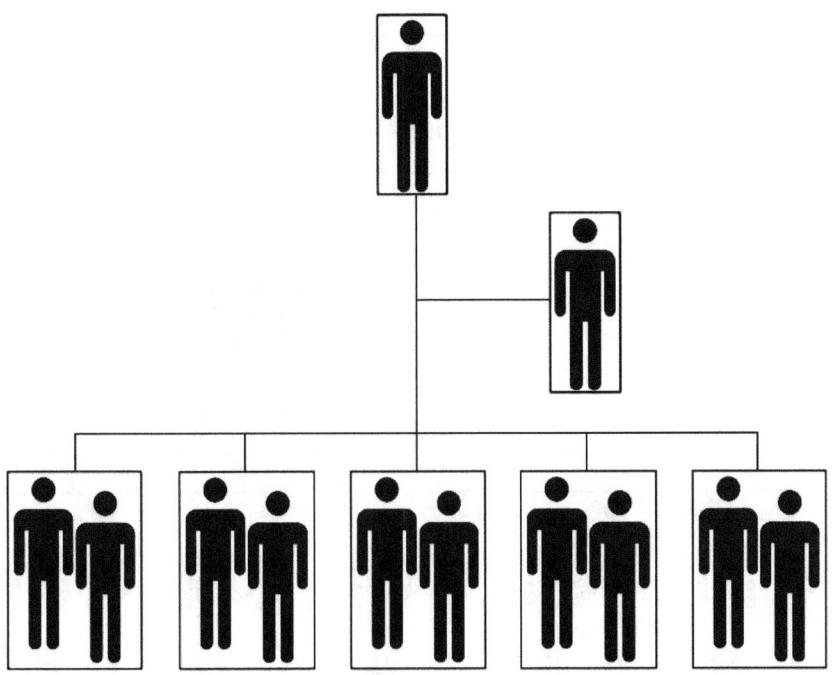

The next step is to shift your Utility Team Leader to your fifth general Team Leader and hire another Helper. A 12 person company can clean up to $47,000 per month.

A 13 Person Company

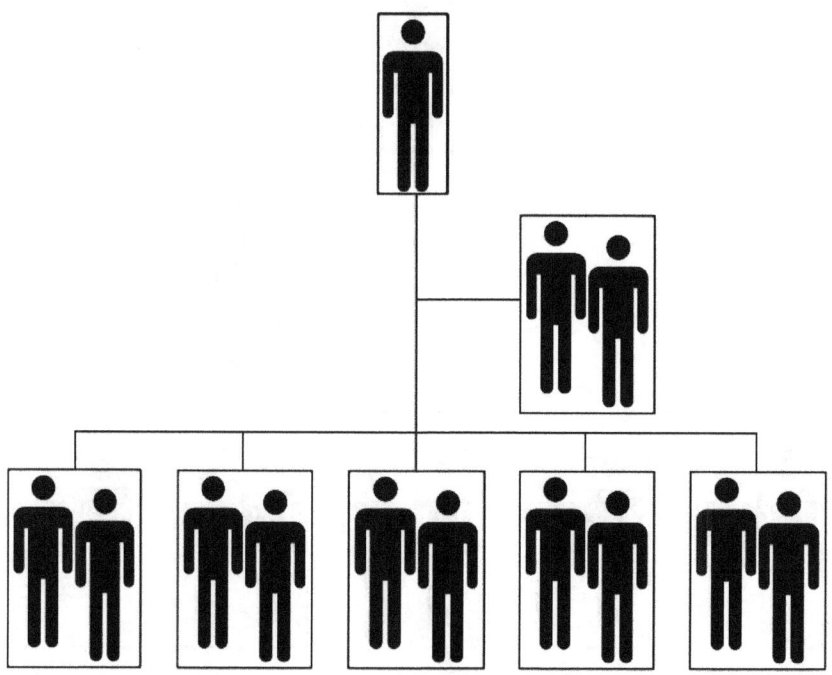

The next step is to promote a helper to Utility Team Leader and hire another Helper. A full time 13 person company can clean up to $49,000 per month.

A 14 Person Company

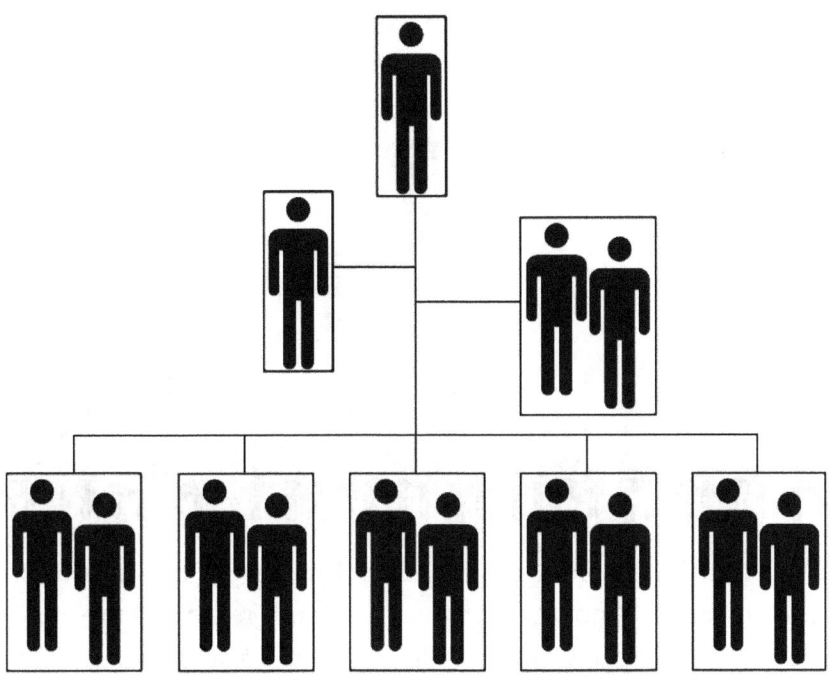

The next step is to hire another Helper to work with you. A 14 person company can clean up to $52,000 per month.

Five general cleaning teams and a utility team is about all that a Unit Manager can effectively handle. This 14 person team is called a unit. The next step in building the business is to promote your best Team Leader to the Unit Manager position.

This will free you up to build another unit.

3 Complete Units

This chart pictures three complete units, each with its own supervisor. A company with 3 complete units can clean up to $150,000 per month.

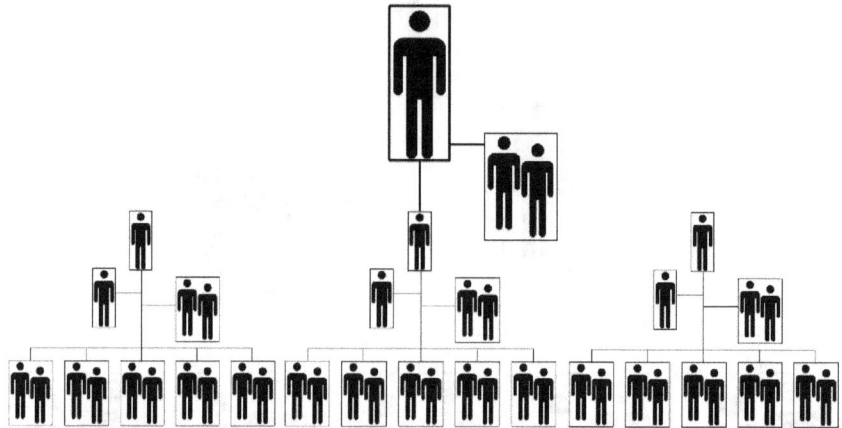

When you have a company this size you can go on vacation for several weeks or months. Eventually you can retire and the money keeps coming in. But you never have to stop growing.

You don't have to stop with one city. You can build as many units in as many different cities or even countries as you want to. How large or small your company becomes depends entirely on you.

It all starts with you and The Ultimate Janitorial Success System; Building one safe step at a time, as slow as you want or as fast as you want. You're the boss.

This lays out the basic business growth plan. As we go through the rest of the seven major ingredients you'll understand more about how all of the different ingredients work together to produce the desired end result.

Things To Remember:

- Define your values and beliefs and put them on paper for you and your team.

- Have a clearly defined job description for each position in your business.

- Have an ascension plan so that good personnel have something to work towards.

- Grow strategically with controlled growth. Build your cleaning capacity by building great system compliant teams.

Chapter 11

CUSTOMER ACQUISITION

The next ingredient on our list of major ingredients is customers. Customers are very important to a business. You have to have customers to have a business.

For most people, the biggest challenge to their janitorial success is simply getting customers. This won't be a problem for you once you understand the simple truth of what janitorial customers really want.

What Do Janitorial Customers Really Want?

To get the answer to this question I commissioned a survey to find out what janitorial customers really wanted. More than 150 facility managers were surveyed. We stopped the survey after 150 because almost everyone gave us the same answer.

This Shouldn't Shock You.

They want better cleaning for their money. They want more hassle free cleaning value!

Surprise, Surprise!

So the question for janitorial contractors is "How do you deliver better cleaning, more value and make more money at the same time? The answer is The Ultimate Janitorial Success System. The next question is how do you get new janitorial clients in order to grow your business?

That question baffles many janitorial business owners. We all know that for a janitorial business to survive, it must be able to get new customers. Believe it or not, getting new customers for your janitorial business is very simple.

I will give you a number of options, any of which will work very well. I know because I use all of them in my business.

We've all heard the expression,

"There Ain't No Free Lunch!"

That phrase reminds us that nothing is really free. Successful companies know that there is a cost involved in getting new customers.

They have that cost figured into their pricing and the way they do business.

McDonalds sells their basic burgers at cost or a slight loss and they make money on sodas, fries and deserts. They spend a lot of money on advertising to get new customers to pay a visit.

All successful companies spend money on getting new customers so you might as well accept that fact and understand that successful businesses of every kind spend money to get new customers. It's called your new customer acquisition cost.

Janitorial Businesses Are No Different

One way or another, you will pay for new janitorial customers. You have 3 choices when it comes to how you choose to acquire janitorial customers. Each method has its advantages and disadvantages.

Your Choices Are:

- Subcontract from another company
- Get Accounts Through Personal Selling
- Hire Your Own Sales Team

#1 Subcontracting:

The easiest and least expensive way to get new customers is to subcontract from a larger janitorial service. When you subcontract, the company you are subcontracting from has spent money on advertising, marketing and sales in order to get the new customer.

You receive less money but you have invested far less into the cost of getting the customer. When you subcontract, the janitorial company you subcontract from is your customer. Another advantage is that they can provide you with several facilities to clean instead of just one.

With a highly efficient systematized cleaning system, that can work in your favor because your labor costs are much lower because the cleaning is accomplished in far less time and with improved quality and consistency.

Within my Janitorial Companies almost all of the Janitorial Services are provided by Subcontractors who have been tested and certified in our cleaning system and use all of the exact products and tools that we specify in our scope of work.

#2 Personal Sales and/or Hiring a Sales Team:

Cleaning is a process. Selling is also a process. There are cleaning tools that make cleaning easier and more effective. There are selling tools that make selling easier and more effective.

Typical Janitorial Sales Funnel

- Develop a good USP.
- Develop a good sales story.
- Acquire a good prospect list.
- Clean and qualify the prospect list.
- Mail the prospect list.
- Call the prospect list.
- Email the prospect list.
- Continue mailing, calling & emailing until you get an appointment.
- Meet with the prospect.
- Tell your story.
- Perform a needs analysis.
- Measure and estimate the time it will take to fulfill the cleaning specifications.
- Prepare a professional looking cleaning proposal.
- Deliver the cleaning proposal and ask for the business.
- Follow up until the prospect buys or ask you to stop calling.

There are selling tools that make the above process somewhat automated by preparing call reports, letters and emails in batches at the appropriate time.

In addition to the selling process and selling tools there are selling skills that can be learned and developed over time.

The important thing to understand is that selling involves a specific process. When this process is followed by people with the right skills and tools then getting new janitorial accounts is not a mystery. It is just a process with very predictable costs and results.

If someone is not interested in learning the process, developing the skills, investing in the tools or hiring sales staff then subcontracting is the best option.

By Subcontracting You Have:

- Lower marketing costs
- One janitorial company can provide you many accounts
- If your service is excellent, they will give you as many accounts as you want.
- If they don't, then you can subcontract from an additional janitorial company too. (Many of our subcontractors were subcontracting from other janitorial companies before subcontracting from us.)
- You don't have to learn the sales game
- You don't have to invest in sales tools, training or personnel
- You don't have to manage professional sales personnel
- You can focus on building great cleaning teams and a great business.

Janitorial Sales and Marketing

In order for you to be able to get new customers, you will need a couple of things. First of all your marketing personnel need to have confidence that you and your team are committed to strictly following your cleaning system without deviation.

When your marketing team is out selling and potential clients ask about your service, show them your cleaning specifications that explain your cleaning system. Our marketing personnel explain that all quality problems are the result of janitorial production system deviation. We explain how our production system eliminates that variation.

If a prospect asks about supervision, we explain that part of our production system. If they ask about equipment we tell them about the equipment that's part of our production system. If they ask about procedure, we tell them about our highly defined and detailed cleaning procedures.

You see, we know our production system works. We know the system is good for the prospective client. There is a reason why we have been given the opportunity to submit a proposal for janitorial services.

The potential client has a cleaning problem. We know that the our cleaning system is the answer to their problem. So to get them to select us, we tell them about the cleaning system and about the good results they'll get. We make promises. In order for us to make these promises convincingly, we need to know that our cleaning teams are committed to keeping those promises.

The second thing you will need is good references. If you're following a strict production system on all of your accounts, those accounts will give good references. If you have good references, you can get lots of new customers. If you have bad references, getting new customers becomes very difficult.

So, your ability to grow has a whole lot to do with the quality and consistency of the cleaning that your teams consistently produce. You also need to realize that if your company is producing poor quality, that will kill your reputation along with your ability to get new customers. Your number one job is to protect the reputation of your business. So, follow a strict cleaning system, produce consistently great services and you'll get all the new customers you want.

Things To Remember:

- Subcontracting is the easiest, safest and least expensive way to get started and grow your cleaning capacity.

- Subcontracting allows you to focus on building great teams.

- Successful janitorial sales and marketing is expensive.

- Successful janitorial sales and marketing is a system with many parts.

- There are marketing tools and strategies that help automate and manage the janitorial marketing process.

GLEN SPRINGFIELD

Chapter 12

LEADERSHIP

The last ingredient I'm going to address is leadership. In your company you must lead by example. Remember the story about the master baker.

No one in your company will work any harder than you do. You have to set the pace and the standards with your example. No one will follow procedures any more than they see you following procedures.

No one will be more honest than they see you being honest. No one will deal with more integrity than they see you dealing with integrity. No one will dress any better than you or smell any better than you for that matter. You have to set the example.

In the beginning of this section of the book I talked about a company philosophy. Every company has one whether it's written down or not. It's determined and communicated through the leadership of the company.

You can write pretty words on paper and read them to everyone, but if you don't live those words, they'll have little impact.

You're Company Vision

To be successful in business, you must have a vision of what you want your company to be. It is up to you to plant that vision in the mind of everyone that works for you and with you. You have to have a mission. You have to be committed to that mission. You have to be determined to take every setback as temporary, and keep on going.

You can be sure there will be set backs and disappointments. How you handle those setbacks and disappointments will determine your future. You'll have many lessons to learn. Some of those lessons will be tough. Some of them may be expensive. But be determined to learn the lessons, and keep on going. Every trial and every lesson contain valuable opportunities to grow in wisdom and character. If you let them, they will make you a smarter and more successful person.

Never stop growing. When you can run, run as fast as you can, when you can only walk, then walk, always going forward, if you can only crawl, then crawl with everything you have.

Never stop growing and never stop moving forward. Be a leader and lead your people to a worthy goal.

Persistence and Determination!

Calvin Coolidge has been often quoted. He was a brilliant and successful man. One of his quotes has stood the test of time and applies as much today as the day he said it. If we understand and apply the message, we will be much closer to the success we seek.

"Nothing in the world can take the place of persistence.

Talent will not; nothing is more common than unsuccessful men with talent.

Genius will not; unrewarded genius is almost a proverb.

Education will not; the world is full of educated derelicts. Persistence and Determination Alone Are Omnipotent."

Perseverance

Steve Jobs the founder of Apple Computer is quoted as saying; *"I'm convinced that about half of what separates the successful entrepreneur from the non-successful ones is pure perseverance."*

Things To Remember:

- Great businesses have great leaders.

- Great leaders have a well-defined vision of where they want the business to go.

- Great leaders are great at helping everyone in their business buy in to their vision.

- Great leaders are persistent and determined.

- Great leaders have grit. Their vision helps them persevere through the trials that come with building a great business.

GLEN SPRINGFIELD

Chapter 13

YOUR 3 BIGGEST DIFFICULTIES

Most Janitorial Businesses Will Ultimately Fail

This chapter explains why . . . and how you can beat the odds, succeeding beyond your wildest dreams!

I don't want to pull any punches as I wrap up this book. I don't want to waste your time, trying to build a successful janitorial business without understanding exactly what you are up against.

My intention is to tell it like it is and I urge you to carefully consider what I'm saying to see if these things are proven by your experiences in your janitorial business or the experiences of those you may know who have their own janitorial business.

I'm going to talk about the 3 biggest difficulties or challenges that you and I have in building a successful, profitable and sustainable business.

These are challenges that every janitorial business owner struggles with. No exceptions. Working solutions for these challenges are not obvious to the majority.

It took me decades of struggling to be able to accurately identify and articulate these challenges. It took me even longer to figure out solutions for each one that actually work.

In this section of the book you will learn in a very short period of time what it took me a few decades of blood, sweat and tears to figure out. Take this information seriously and you will leap ahead of your competition and create the business and the lifestyle that you originally intended when you started your janitorial business.

Big Opportunity

There is lots of opportunity in the janitorial business. Billions of dollars are spent every year cleaning offices and restrooms. There are thousands of janitorial services in every major city providing these services.

Why Do The Majority Fail?

Sad to say but most of these janitorial services will never be nearly as successful as they could be. Most will get stuck at a very small size or they will simply cease to exist. Why?

The reason is that they never figure out how to overcome these 3 major obstacles to their janitorial success. In this section of the book we will identify the 3 Biggest Difficulties that Janitorial Contractors face and show you how each of these difficulties can become a **strategic advantage** for you.

When you overcome these difficulties you can build a highly successful janitorial business you can be proud of. If you fail to overcome these 3 difficulties you are doomed to a lot of frustration and struggle.

The 3 Biggest Difficulties:

The first major difficulty is Janitorial Marketing. That is simply getting janitorial accounts to clean. Most janitorial contractors never make it over this first hurdle.

Marketing is both a science and an art. Few that start their own janitorial businesses have an accurate concept of what is involved in marketing janitorial services.

It doesn't take them long to figure out that new janitorial customers aren't that easy to acquire especially if you don't know what you are doing.

The old concept that if you invent a better mousetrap the world will beat a path to your door is a very flawed concept.

The world has to first become aware of the possibility that a better mousetrap is possible.

Then they must agree that the better mousetrap really offers valuable benefits over a conventional mouse trap and that any additional cost are offset by a mountain of benefits.

If you believe that you are entitled to new janitorial customers for your business just because you intend on delivering great janitorial services then you are in for a very unpleasant reality check.

It simply doesn't work that way. All janitorial services claim to deliver great janitorial services. No one claims or even admits that their janitorial services are inferior.

Claiming that you will deliver great service is not a marketing advantage or solution to the Janitorial Marketing challenge.

Those janitorial contractors who finally make it over the janitorial marketing hurdle and figure out how to get customers get hammered by the next two difficulties.

Difficulty #2: Low Profit Margin

The second major difficulty is low production rates and low profits.

This is where a particular janitorial account may have been bid at and would be profitable with a cleaning production rate of 6500 square feet per hour but you or your cleaning crew is cleaning at a production rate of 4000 sq. ft. per man hour to fulfill the specifications.

This means that your labor cost is eating up all of the profits leaving you nothing for your time and effort.

The Third Major Difficulty:

Quality Control / Account Retention

The third major difficulty is keeping your janitorial accounts and keeping them happy. This is accomplished with "better than average" quality control.

When janitorial business owners are doing all of the cleaning themselves, they are controlling the quality. The problem begins when the janitorial business owner is not onsite and inspecting the work each night.

When they hand the job of maintaining quality standards over to someone else, then the quality of services delivered can quickly become a problem that leads to constant complaints, lost accounts and a lots of frustration.

The Perfect Scenario

If you could get all of the janitorial accounts you want, if you could get them cleaned at high production rates and if you could maintain A+ quality control then that would be pretty sweet - Right?

If that's what you are interested in then read on.

The Root Causes Of These Difficulties

In order to craft certain solutions for these three difficulties we need to look at their root causes. If we can address the root causes then the difficulties will be eliminated.

The first difficulty is getting janitorial accounts. To understand this problem, we need to put ourselves in the shoes of a janitorial decision maker.

Facility Managers or Purchasing Agents have probably hired a dozen different janitorial services over the years. Each service promised great service. Each service started out doing a good job but then service declined with time.

After a while the janitorial decision maker gets tired of complaining.

They've had enough.

They take bids and go through the process of selecting a new janitorial service provider. As they interview new potential janitorial services they hear the same old promises that they have always heard and the cycle repeats.

The "Yellow Pencil" Syndrome

As Janitorial Service Business Owners we have a big problem. That problem is how do we look different or better than all of the other janitorial services?

In the Dallas Texas market area, building managers and purchasing agents have 3,000 plus janitorial services to choose from. If you were in their shoes, which one would you choose? They all look the same. They all sound the same. They all make the same promises.

They all provide the same services. It's like selecting a yellow pencil from a pile of 3,000 yellow pencils. Which yellow pencil would you choose?

The answer from most is that it doesn't really matter. That's how most janitorial decision makers really feel. They believe that all janitorial services are basically the same, making and breaking the same promises.

Another Lesson From the Fast Food Industry

To overcome the biggest Janitorial Marketing Challenge, you have to create a "unique product" – a cleaning service that is different than all of the other cleaning services in the market place.

If you ask someone what their favorite fast food hamburger is you will get a lot of different answers for a lot of different reasons. The point to notice is that all of the various hamburger products are significantly different in ways that a portion of the market favors.

The big fast food franchises spend a lot of time, money and effort to distinguish their products as different. If Burger King, Wendy's, McDonald's and Whataburger all had the exact same products, it wouldn't really matter where you went to buy a burger. Each hamburger shop would have nothing unique to offer or sell. As a customer – you wouldn't care where you went for your burgers.

Janitorial decision makers are the same way. They don't care much which janitorial service they choose because all janitorial services look the same to them. They provide the same services and make the same promises.

Until you have a unique cleaning service to offer, you will be lost in an ocean of "yellow pencil" janitorial services with no way to get the attention of potential janitorial customers.

Creating a unique janitorial service that will receive favor from a portion of the janitorial market is not as complicated as you might think. We did it with our S.M.A.R.T. Office Cleaning System and Demonstration. You can get a few clues about our system by checking out our website at www.deltajanitorial.com.

The Second Major Difficulty Is
Low Production Rates And Low Profits

Most cleaning crews are using old cleaning technology and old cleaning strategies to clean their janitorial accounts. These companies experience production rates of 3500 to 5000 sq. ft. per man hour, averaging in the low 4000 range.

New cleaning strategies, products and tools utilizing new technology is producing production rates of 6000 to 7000 sq. ft. per man hour. The cleaning personnel are cleaning more area in less time. They're doing a better, a more consistent job with less effort and less fatigue.

Most janitorial companies are still using a cleaning strategy known as "area cleaning" where one person does all of the cleaning in a designated area. That "area" could be a small office building or a few floors of a multistory building.

Using the Area Cleaning Strategy, each cleaning person will take care of a certain "area". Their duties will including removing the trash, vacuuming the carpet, cleaning the restrooms, performing the dusting duties, mopping the hard surface floors, plus all of the miscellaneous cleaning duties in that particular area.

A good production rate for area cleaning is 3,000 to 4,000 square feet per hour. A strategy that is proven to be far more efficient is called Team Cleaning.

In this strategy the duties are split up to where the work is accomplished by a team of specialist, with each member of the team responsible for duties that are associated with their specialized tool set.

The smallest team is a two person team with the first person taking care of all of the cleaning above the floor in a single pass through the building. The second person does the vacuuming and mopping while checking the work of the first person. Using the Team

Cleaning strategy, production rates are in the 6,000 to 7,500 sq. ft. per man hour range.

Assembly Line Cleaning

Team Cleaning takes the benefits that come from an assembly line where different workers specialize in completing a portion of the total product. Since the workers specialize, they are more efficient and produce fewer defects.

A second reason for low production rates is old technology. Most janitorial service providers are using the same tools and products that were commonly used decades ago.

New technology has made cleaning easier and faster, if you are aware of and use the new technology. Pretreated cloths and pretreated mops alone produce a whopping 65% improvement in productivity.

High tech dusters, vacuums and other tools speed things up even more.

It is very hard to compete with janitorial service providers who average cleaning rates of 6500 sq. ft. per man hour while your cleaning crews can only average cleaning rates of 4000 sq. ft. per man hour.

Creating a modern and efficient cleaning system that utilizes new technology will deliver more thorough cleaning, along with much faster cleaning production rates.

Labor is and always will be the largest expense in the delivery of cleaning services. That is why even small improvements in productivity achieved through better products and tools deliver high returns on investment.

Cleaning production rates are being improved so much through technology that very soon those that do not adopt systemization and new technology will be squeezed out of the janitorial business altogether.

The Third Major Difficulty: Account Retention

The third major difficulty is poor quality control and inconsistent cleaning resulting in dirty buildings, customer complaints and lost janitorial accounts.

Most janitorial providers try to control quality through inspecting completed work. While that strategy may work for "one-time" jobs like post construction clean-up and event cleaning, it doesn't work well for routine janitorial services.

It's economically impossible to check every detail of the cleaning of every cleaning service. The cost of inspection is too high.

Even Another Lesson From The Fast Food Industry

Everyone knows that fast food franchises crank out consistent products. Each hamburger looks and tastes just like all of the other hamburgers made that day, that week and that month.

You will note that this consistency is not produced because each hamburger is inspected by a hamburger inspector before it is given to a customer.

The consistency comes from the fact that each franchise has a system for producing their product. That system is strictly defined. There is no guesswork involved. The system allows for very little variation.

Fast food products are produced very efficiently with the most modern equipment. As long as their system is followed, the resulting products have almost no variation. The production system is like a cookie cutter that cranks out identical products, time after time.

Poor and inconsistent quality in janitorial cleaning is caused by variation in the tools, products and processes used by cleaning personnel.

Most janitorial providers do not have a highly defined methodology for providing their services.

When variations are removed from cleaning processes then variation is removed from the cleaning result. Janitorial service providers can learn a lot from the fast food franchises.

Fast food products are very consistent. Fast food franchisors have created strict systems for how their products are made with the goal of creating a consistent product that the market will keep coming back for.

If the product becomes inconsistent then the market will quit coming back.

Using new technology in tools and processes plus the team cleaning strategy produces more consistent cleaning at much faster production rates. However, not all cleaning personnel will embrace this kind of "zero variation" cleaning strategy.

Some people are very resistant to change and to adopting new systems. They want to do things their own way or however they perceive is the easiest way to get the job done. Don't let these people ruin your business.

If you want to work at Burger King, you have to follow the Burger King system and do things the Burger King way. If you don't – you get fired.

The same is true for staff at all of the major fast food franchises. You either strictly follow their systems or you get fired quickly. System resistant personnel are not tolerated.

Don't put up with system resistant people in your business. They are difficult, they waste your time and they waste your money.

The 3 Biggest Difficulties To Janitorial Success

1. Getting Janitorial Accounts - Creating a unique janitorial service that is favored by a segment of the janitorial market.

2. Achieving high cleaning production rates and profits.

3. Creating a system that produces consistent, zero variation cleaning through staff.

What Happens To Janitorial Services When These Difficulties Are Not Resolved?

Consider how many have set out to build a successful janitorial business.

- Most janitorial businesses never even get off the ground. They may never even get their first account.

- Other janitorial businesses get stuck and stay very small.

- Almost all janitorial businesses make far less profit than they should.

- Almost all janitorial businesses lose far more accounts than they should.

- Almost all janitorial business owners get stuck, frantically working "in" their janitorial business, working harder than their staff, never having the time to enjoy the benefits of being the owner.

The Three Core Advantages

Your successful janitorial business begins with a unique cleaning service that is different than most other janitorial services in a way that is favored by a portion of the janitorial market.

You must have something unique to offer or you become one of the thousands of other "yellow pencil" janitorial services.

Once you have a Unique Service to offer you will have a Unique Product Advantage.

There are two more business advantages you want to add to your business. After you have a solid Unique Product Advantage, you will need a system to deliver your unique janitorial services as quickly and as consistently as possible so that your production rates are high and your labor costs are low.

Your system must utilize every technological and strategic advantage available so that no one can deliver your unique cleaning service better or faster than you can. This will give you a Production/Delivery Advantage. That is the second business advantage you want over the competition.

Your delivery system must be highly defined so that you can diligently root out the variation and system resistance that is the root cause of inconsistent cleaning and lost accounts.

Add to this a way to monitor system compliance and you have a Quality Consistency Advantage. This is the third business advantage that will make your business bulletproof.

In short, you have to do in your janitorial business, all of the things that Fast Food Franchisors have done to make their products unique, valuable and consistent.

Things To Remember:

- There are three big difficulties you face in building a great janitorial business.
    - Making your services unique and more desirable than others.
    - Delivering your services more efficiently than others.
    - Managing the consistency of your services better than others.
- Each of the three difficulties can be turned into strategic advantages when your solutions to these difficulties are perfected.

Chapter 14

UJSS CONCLUSION

In this book, I've repeatedly and consistently made many comparisons between operating a successfully janitorial business and operating a successful fast food franchise. There is good reason for that. I believe that what has happened within the fast food industry is a very good predictor of what will happen within the commercial cleaning industry very soon.

At one time the fast food industry didn't exist in the same way that it does now. Hamburgers and french-fries were made and served mostly by family owned establishments who operated their businesses without the benefit of production systems and new technology.

They used old family recipes and operated much like the generation before. There was very little innovation.

And Then The World Began To Change . . .

Then along came McDonalds and everything began to change quickly. Systems were created so that fewer workers could serve more customers. Systems were strictly defined and enforced so that variation was virtually eliminated from the production of their products.

New systems were designed to eliminate wasted food and to lower food costs. Existing systems were improved with even better and more sophisticated technology. Systems got better and better. Equipment improved making it possible for even a smaller staff to be able to serve even more customers with even more consistent products.

The Good Old Days Faded Away

It wasn't long before the mom and pop hamburger joints all but disappeared. The "old ways" couldn't compete with systemization and technology. Owners either had to adopt systemization and new technology to lower their own production costs or go broke fighting a battle they couldn't win with the old ways of doing business.

New fast-food franchises popped up with their own unique products and systematized ways of producing consistent quality at very competitive prices. Technology, innovation, systemization and continuous improvement continue to drive these businesses.

Escalating Startup Costs

At one time, the cost to open a hamburger joint was comparatively low. All you needed was a location and a small commercial kitchen.

Now the cost of entry is much higher with fast food franchises costing hundreds of thousands and even millions of dollars for a single location.

People are lined up to buy these franchises because the return on investment is so high. Systemization, innovation and technology changed this industry to the point that small operators can't compete and the cost to enter this business is now beyond the reach of most people.

Today, the cost of entry into the janitorial business is still relatively small. It is within the reach of most people. It won't stay that way much longer.

The janitorial industry is undergoing the same massive change that began in the fast food industry several decades ago. Most people are unaware of what is happening around them.

New janitorial technology, new tools, systemization and innovation are lowering labor costs and raising the bar for quality control.

The change is already underway. The janitorial industry will experience a massive growth in systemization and profits as cleaning processes are refined and improved. The new technology will require a greater investment but labor cost will shrink making way for greater profits.

The cost of entry into the janitorial business will continue to rise along with profits and rising returns on investment.

Those who are in the janitorial business now have the opportunity to adopt new technology and systemize their processes now while it is still relatively affordable.

Those who refuse to invest in new technology will be forced out of business by those with lower labor costs and higher profits.

The Handwriting Is On The Wall!

The handwriting is on the wall for janitorial business owners. Everyone who wants to succeed in the janitorial business needs to take note of how fast technology and innovation is changing janitorial production rates and how fast systemization is redefining quality control.

In this section of the book we have identified the three biggest difficulties that janitorial contractors face in building a successful janitorial business. We have then prescribed the one and only solution for overcoming each of these difficulties.

These difficulties are not made up or imagined. Ask anyone who has or who is trying to build a successful janitorial business. They will confirm the validity of the information in this book.

These are really big problems for most janitorial contractors. These are the challenges that will prevent most janitorial businesses from reaching their full potential. But it's not all bad.

Those that embrace and apply the principles of TQM (Total Quality Management), systemization, innovation and new technology will find amazing opportunity in the janitorial industry.

Most in the janitorial industry are unaware of the trends we've discussed in this book and the impact they are sure to have. They think they are doing OK with their current cleaning production rates and their current methodologies.

When they begin losing clients to companies that have been built on these principles, they will find it very difficult to catch up. Most won't be able to compete.

But you have been blessed with this information while there is still time to learn it and apply it in your janitorial business.

With your janitorial business built on the solid foundation of the principles discussed in this book, your production rates will soar, your labor costs will decrease, your quality control will increase along with your profits.

You will become stronger and more competitive, delivering greater and greater value to your clientele.

The Ultimate Janitorial Success System

It's pretty easy to see that if you have a Unique Product Advantage, a Production/Delivery Advantage and a Quality Consistency Advantage that you can build a solid, stable janitorial business and probably become the dominate janitorial service in your area.

With these Three Advantages, how could you not succeed? Right?

However, the Three Advantages come with three pretty difficult challenges.

1. Challenge #1: How do you take a service like janitorial services and make them unique in a way that a significant segment of the market will prefer over all of the others? In this short book you've read how I did it.

2. Challenge #2: How can you deliver your janitorial services in a unique way that your customers will perceive as an advantage to them?

3. Challenge #3: How can you monitor cleaning system compliance in multiple remote locations and explain your process in a way that seems advantageous to your customer?

When you have overcome these three challenges, you will be unstoppable. It will take more than a little effort but the payoff will be huge!

GLEN SPRINGFIELD

Chapter 15

JANITORIAL BUSINESS COACHING

For some reason people are hesitant to ask for help or to let the world know that they don't have all the answers. They don't want others to know that they don't know how to do something or that they don't know how to get something done. Perhaps they will feel embarrassed.

Real professionals don't have this problem. High performance professional athletes all have coaches. From Tiger Woods to Olympic hopefuls, they achieve higher performance through being coached. The fact is, they would never have achieved the levels of success they have without being coached.

High performance business executives and entrepreneurs also need and use coaches. When an entrepreneur is really focused on self-improvement and moving projects forward quickly, they look for all the help they can get. A different perspective often produces amazing breakthroughs.

When an entrepreneur works with a coach, their path to success is much shorter and more likely. Here is some information and statistics I got from ICF (International Coach Foundation).

Benefits of Business Coaching

1. Increased Productivity. Professional coaching maximizes potential and therefore, unlocks latent sources of productivity.

    a. 70% Improvement in Work Performance

    b. 61% Improvement in Business Management

    c. 57% Improvement in Time Management

    d. 51% Improvement in Team Effectiveness

2. Positive People. Building self-confidence to face challenges is critical to success.

    a. 80% Improvement in Self-Confidence

    b. 73% Improved Relationships

    c. 72% Improved Communication Skills

    d. 67% Improved Life/Work Balance

3. Return on Investment. Coaching generates learning and clarity for forward action with a commitment to measurable outcomes. The vast majority of companies (86%) say they at least made their investment back.

4. Satisfied Clients. Virtually all companies and individuals who hire a coach are satisfied.

    a. 99% are Somewhat or Very Satisfied

b. 96% Would Repeat the Process

Just like a good tool, a good coach pays for himself many times over. When you are building a business, you will face lots of challenges you don't know how to handle.

If you can take your challenges to a knowledgeable coach who is committed to helping you achieve your goals, then your chances of success will have increased enormously.

If you would like to learn more about Janitorial Business Coaching or if you just want some help developing your own Unique Product Advantage, your own Production/Delivery Advantage and your own Quality Consistency Advantage, I have a very special offer for you.

"Free 20 Minute Consulting Call Plus Free 30 Day Trial Membership In the Association of Janitorial and Cleaning Contractors (AJACC) Inner Circle Valued At $319.95"

Myself or one of our Janitorial Business Coaches will speak with you personally to answer your questions about starting or expanding your own Dream Janitorial Business so you can begin building your janitorial business at lightening-speed, amaze your family and friends, and once and for all shut up all the critics who have ever predicted your failure and said "you couldn't do it."

Email TheJanicoach@gmail.com. In the Subject line write: Request for Consulting Call. We will contact you to arrange a mutually convenient time where we can discuss your business, your goals and options and help you put together your plan. Together, we'll figure out the best action plan for you and your situation.

I wish you the all best in achieving your janitorial business building goals. If my team and I can help, give us a call.

GLEN SPRINGFIELD

Chapter 16

HOW WELL DO YOU SLEEP ON STORMY NIGHTS?

I want to wrap this book up with a story that I found very helpful. Use it and you too will sleep well on stormy nights.

Once there was a farmer who decided he wanted to hire a farm hand. The work was getting a little too much for him and his wife, so he wanted to hire someone to help out. He ran an ad in the local paper for a farm hand. Well only one young man applied for the job. This disappointed the farmer because the young man looked a little green and inexperienced.

The farmer asks the young applicant if he had ever operated any farm equipment. The young man replied "no, I've never operated any farm equipment, but I can sleep on stormy nights."

The farmer looked puzzled and asked "Have you ever been around farm animals?" The young man replied "No sir I haven't, but I can sleep like a baby on stormy nights."

The farmer looked even more puzzled and asked "have you ever done any gardening?" The young man confidently reported "No sir, I haven't, but no matter how hard the wind blows, I can sleep on stormy nights."

The farmer asked "Have you ever even visited a farm before?" The young man said "No sir, I haven't, but sir, no matter how bright the lightening or how loud the thunder, I can sleep on stormy nights.

The farmer was perplexed. He wanted a hand, but this boy didn't appear to be exactly suited for the job. Since this was the only applicant the farmer decided to give the boy a chance. He showed him to the bunk house and told the boy he could start in the morning.

Well, the boy turned out to be a quick learner, and a pretty good hand. One night, a few weeks later, after everyone had gone to bed, a terrible storm came up. The wind was blowing, lightening was flashing and the thunder was deafening. The farmer jumped out of bed, threw on his slicker, and headed outside.

First he headed for the hay pile to put a tarp over it. When he got there it was already covered. Next he headed for the tractor to put it in the barn. He found it was already in the barn. Then he headed for the corral to put the horses up. They were already put up. Everything he went to do was already done. He headed for the bunk house and woke up the young man. He said "Did you cover the hay, put the tractor and the horses up, and secure all the shutters and all the other stuff?" The young man just looked at him and said "Of course I did, I told you that I could sleep in stormy nights."

My hope and wish for all of you, is that you too, will be able to sleep like a baby on the stormiest of nights.

ABOUT THE AUTHOR

Glen began his cleaning business as a window cleaner more than 40 years ago cleaning retail store fronts. Over the years his business evolved from a simple window cleaning service into a full service janitorial business. It took more than 15 years for Glen's business to reach a million dollars in sales, providing a comfortable lifestyle. That suddenly came to an end when Glen lost his business in a divorce.

To survive financially he quickly started another janitorial business. This time things were quite different. This second janitorial business reached over a million dollars in sales in only nine months, growing to over six million in annual sales over the next five years.

Glen attributes his success to an unusual commitment to personal self-improvement and targeted education. Although he never finished high school, Glen is an avid consumer of success and business information.

He invests in books, courses and seminars, spending thousands of dollars each year on the best information available. This supplies his businesses with fresh ideas helping his teams reach higher and higher levels of success. Glen learned that while poor people have big TV's, rich people have big libraries.

www.ingramcontent.com/pod-product-compliance
Lightning Source LLC
Chambersburg PA
CBHW071436180526
45170CB00001B/361